Wildlands of the West

Wildlands
of the West

THE STORY OF
THE BUREAU OF LAND MANAGEMENT

BY LESLIE ALLEN   PHOTOGRAPHED BY MELISSA FARLOW

NATIONAL GEOGRAPHIC
WASHINGTON, D.C.

CONTENTS

LEFT: In autumn's vanguard, aspens gild slopes of the San Juan Mountains in Colorado, where BLM terrain scales 14,000-foot peaks. PREVIOUS PAGES: Erin "Red" Thompson makes music in a balancing act during the annual Burning Man artfest in Nevada's Black Rock Desert. PAGE ONE: Ranchers race the sun on a BLM allotment near Moab, in southeastern Utah.

A WESTERN MOSAIC

THE BUREAU OF LAND MANAGEMENT HOLDINGS

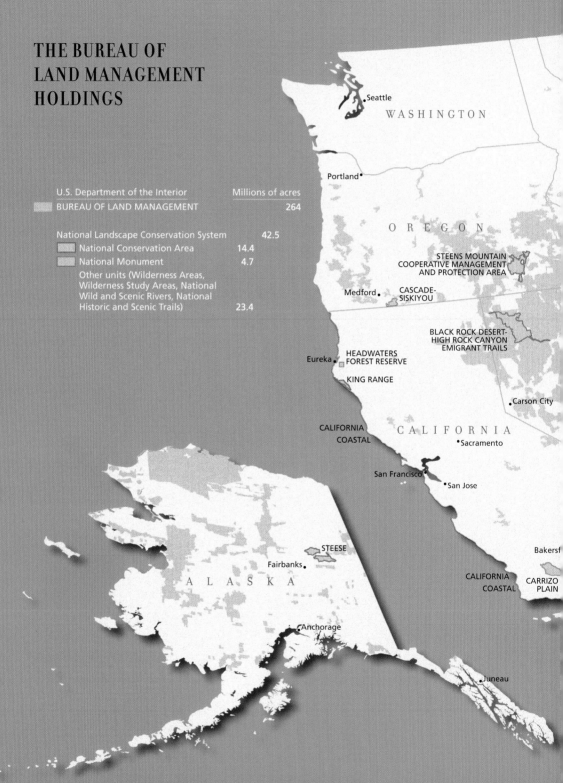

U.S. Department of the Interior	Millions of acres
BUREAU OF LAND MANAGEMENT	264
National Landscape Conservation System	42.5
National Conservation Area	14.4
National Monument	4.7
Other units (Wilderness Areas, Wilderness Study Areas, National Wild and Scenic Rivers, National Historic and Scenic Trails)	23.4

Seattle

WASHINGTON

Portland

OREGON

STEENS MOUNTAIN COOPERATIVE MANAGEMENT AND PROTECTION AREA

Medford

CASCADE-SISKIYOU

BLACK ROCK DESERT-HIGH ROCK CANYON EMIGRANT TRAILS

Eureka

HEADWATERS FOREST RESERVE

KING RANGE

Carson City

CALIFORNIA COASTAL

CALIFORNIA

Sacramento

San Francisco

San Jose

STEESE

Fairbanks

Bakersf

ALASKA

CALIFORNIA COASTAL

CARRIZO PLAIN

Anchorage

Juneau

NORTH DAKOTA

MINNESOTA

UPPER MISSOURI RIVER BREAKS

Great Falls

M O N T A N A

Helena

Billings

POMPEYS PILLAR

SOUTH DAKOTA

I D A H O

se

CRATERS OF THE MOON

Pocatello

W Y O M I N G

NEBRASKA

SNAKE RIVER BIRDS OF PREY

Cheyenne

KANSAS

Salt Lake City

Denver

N E V A D A

U T A H

C O L O R A D O

COLORADO CANYONS

GUNNISON GORGE

CANYONS OF THE ANCIENTS

GRAND STAIRCASE-ESCALANTE

TEXAS

VERMILION CLIFFS

KASHA-KATUWE TENT ROCKS

Santa Fe

RED ROCK CANYON

Las Vegas

GRAND CANYON-PARASHANT

Albuquerque

EL MALPAIS

Flagstaff

NEW MEXICO

A R I Z O N A

CALIFORNIA DESERT

CONSERVATION AREA

AGUA FRIA

Palm Springs

SANTA ROSA AND SAN JACINTO MOUNTAINS

Los Angeles

Phoenix

GILA BOX RIPARIAN

SONORAN DESERT

IRONWOOD FOREST

Tucson

SAN PEDRO RIPARIAN

San Diego

LAS CIENEGAS

Scale varies in this perspective.

"THE LANDS NO ONE KNOWS"

Room enough to get lost.

More, much more than enough. Deep within southern Utah's heart of stone, I'm roaming the San Rafael Swell, a 1,500-square-mile dome that's been folded, chiseled, and swept into mesas and slot canyons, bronzed badlands, and razorback reefs. In concentric circles, like frozen pond ripples, colorful rock formations move backward through time to the Swell's geological center, where perennial desert streams scour canyon walls of 250-million-year-old Permian sandstone.

I never get anywhere near them.

First, my map shows a route that turns out to be a 300-foot drop over a cliff face. Time to take a deep breath, curse the mapmaker, reconsider the route. An hour or two later, in my car, I am at a fork in the road, face-to-face with my choices: a slope of gleaming slickrock or a boulder-strewn gully. Not that my vehicle could transit either one of them—or the stream I unexpectedly find myself at while recalling Swell stories I've heard about abandoned cars, sunstruck forced marches to distant roads, and the like.

Room enough to get lost. With its one-two punch of promise—lots of room—and peril—getting lost—this phrase has been echoing in my city-dweller's mind ever since I came west from Washington, D.C., a few weeks ago. My assignment seemed straightforward: to explore and

In southern Utah, among other places, you can bypass famous sights and focus on the parallel universe of BLM lands without feeling slighted.

report on the U.S. Bureau of Land Management's huge but little known domain. Lately, though, I find myself being drawn farther and farther into some pretty wild territory. Room enough to get lost: It's turning into a siren call.

You could get yourself extremely lost here in the San Rafael Swell, a fact not wasted on the likes of the outlaw Butch Cassidy, or the posses who ate his dust deep within the Swell. (After today, I also understand why so many UFO enthusiasts say alien beings hang out in these landscapes, so otherworldly.) For better or worse, nobody has crossed my path all day. But eventually, Factory Butte, a soaring limestone battleship crowned by a medieval fortress, sails back into view, pointing the way to pavement.

In 1936, conservationist Bob Marshall identified some two million acres of wilderness within the San Rafael Swell. Increasingly threatened by development and abuse from off-road vehicles since his time, the Swell nevertheless remains one of the nation's largest, grandest desert areas. Nowadays, Utahns may know the Swell, but outlanders still tend not to. Thousands of tourists speed right by on connect-the-dot auto tours of canyon country's marquee names—nearby national parks like Zion, Bryce, Arches, Canyonlands, and Capitol Reef, which partly adjoins the San Rafael Swell. They don't have a clue about what they're missing.

For drop-dead scenery, wildlife, plant life, archaeology, or history, the Swell is a sleeper. For solitude, it beats its five-star neighbors hands down. To some extent, the San Rafael Swell is just a face in the crowd, one among dozens of spectacular places administered by the Bureau of Land Management (BLM).

Millions of acres of spectacle…. Within a couple of hours by car from the Swell, for instance, are the Book Cliffs, where large elk herds roam under one of the world's longest escarpments. Also nearby, but on the opposite end of the size spectrum, are the little pre-Columbian figures that peer from shadowy walls where the Green River folds itself into bowknots in Labyrinth Canyon. Or—a personal favorite—Lockhart Basin, a ragged sea of cliffs, pinnacles, buttes, and canyons, subject to remodeling by each passing cloud shadow. Stippled or striped, its rusts, creams, turquoises, and other hues are sometimes subtle, sometimes bold. Lockhart isn't exactly a household name, though a BLM employee in nearby Moab told me of visitors who rank its vistas with the Grand Canyon's. In southern Utah, among other places, you can bypass famous sights and focus on the parallel universe of BLM lands without feeling slighted.

BLM's expanses used to be known as "the lands no one wanted" or "the leftover lands," ironically. After homesteads, land grants, Indian reservations, states, railroad companies, national parks, forests, refuges, and military installations all took a share of the public domain, these were the lands, mainly in the West, that remained under federal ownership. In 1946, the BLM came into existence to manage them for sometimes conflicting uses. The agency administers public grazing lands where more than 20,000 ranchers run cattle and other livestock. It leases several hundred thousand oil, gas, coal, and geothermal sites and hundreds of thousands of gold and other hardrock mineral claims. It manages commercial timberlands, oversees millions of acres valued for their ancient artifacts or their fossils, and manages its lands for the scenic and natural values that people seek out as well. The domain is "rich in a spectrum of resources," said one (CONTINUED ON PAGE 24)

FOLLOWING PAGES:
Sunlight finds a quiet trough amid a choppy sea of rock and ice in southwestern Colorado. Trails blasted by early miners became the present-day Alpine Loop, a BLM byway best explored by four-wheel-drive vehicle.

Sea lions sprawl across an offshore outcropping, one among thousands of exposed Pacific reefs, rocks, islands, and pinnacles joined into BLM's California Coastal National Monument. Ashore (opposite), deeply folded slopes of the rain-swept King Range soar above the Lost Coast. North of Shelter Cove, hikers can labor to the top of 4,088-foot King Peak for fog-free ocean views.

FOLLOWING PAGES:

String of wild horses stitches Wyoming's Red Desert beneath the Honeycomb Buttes. Seeming barrenness belies the area's importance as a habitat for some 350 wildlife species, including pronghorn antelope: One of the world's largest herds lives here.

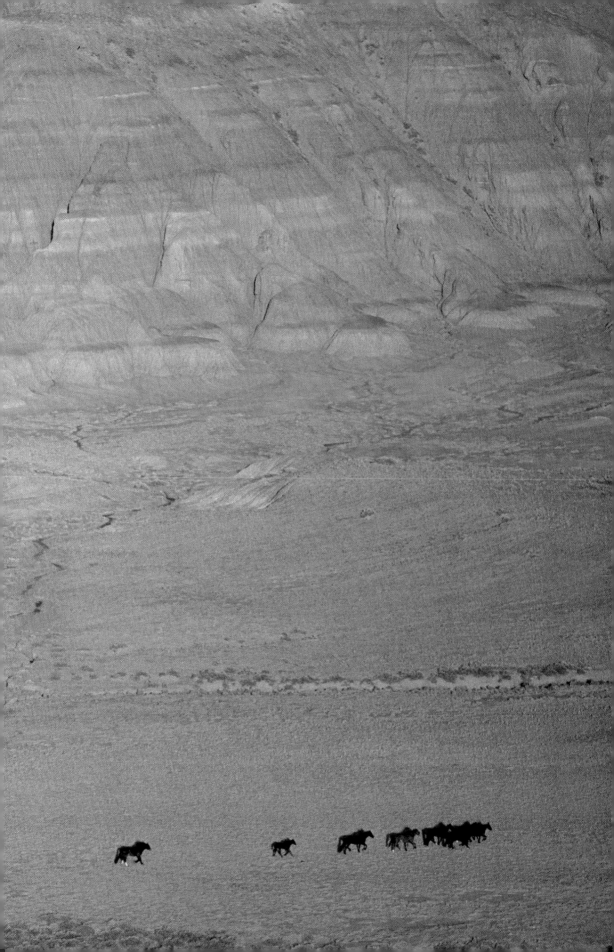

A lone cyclist crosses the
maritime chaparral of Fort
Ord, once a bustling Army post
on central California's
Monterey Peninsula and now a
BLM-run reserve for scarce
native habitats.

FOLLOWING PAGES:
Privately owned river bottom
carries the flow that nourishes
lush public land above Idaho's
Medicine Lodge Creek. Private
and state inholdings remain
more prevalent in BLM's
domain than on other
federal lands.

conservationist, "from the wilderness that illuminates the spirit to the coal that lights a city."

The agency's outsized task begins with the land itself. For superlatives, start with size: more than 262 million acres, including 85 million in Alaska. That adds up to almost an eighth of the nation's landmass. For comparison's sake, BLM's holdings are more than triple the National Park Service's 84 million acres. They far exceed even Forest Service holdings, totaling 192 million acres. But given all its elbowroom, the BLM commands infinitesimal name recognition. "The bureau of what?" asked several well-meaning acquaintances when I first told them the subject of this book.

"Who owns all this?" my son Ethan wants to know as we pass the hours one day moving west, then north, along Nevada's lonely highways. The open rangeland is utterly unpeopled, bounded only by low, parallel ranges that rise up like waves in the sagebrush sea. Today, summer lightning is dancing across the ridgetops, putting on a show for us, sparking outliers of the big blazes burning farther to the north. Here and there in these ranges are places only a few people have ever seen: stream-cut caves big enough to float a raft through, a thousand-foot-high waterfall, and other surprises.

I tell him that he owns the sagebrush flats and the secret caves and hot springs and the rest of it, and I do, and so do all Americans. But direct evidence is lacking. The BLM keeps a low profile, posting few signs in its domain, putting forth no mascots like the Forest Service's Smokey to tell us where we are and how we should care for it. So we unfold our maps, the kind that show in detail land ownership in the western states. White patches indicate private land and light blue stands for state holdings; forests, of course, are green. Yellow, the BLM color, spills across the map. Nevada is awash in yellow, to the tune of almost 48 million acres, more than two-

Prowlike Pilot Rock—a plug of volcanic basalt—juts 400 feet above Cascade-Siskiyou National Monument, a crossroads of mountain ranges, geological eras, and habitats in southern Oregon. Mt. Shasta rises in the far distance, across the state line in California.

thirds of the state. A bit under half of Utah, nearly 23 million acres, falls under BLM's jurisdiction. Moving down the list, a little less than a third of Wyoming, some 18 million acres, is managed by BLM; more than a fourth of Oregon and about a fifth of Arizona fall within the agency's domain. In the West, California, Idaho, Montana, Washington, New Mexico, and Colorado all have sizable BLM holdings (and there are even some yellow glints far east of the 100th meridian, like Arkansas' 6,000 acres).

Between the Rockies and the Pacific, one in every five acres is BLM yellow. There, the color of sunshine tells the classic western story of cloudless skies, little rainfall, and iffy cropland in the rain shadows that define most of the region. Here in central Nevada, in the heart of the Great Basin, fewer than eight inches of rain fall in an average year. The Mojave and Sonoran Deserts, to the southwest, get even less moisture. The steppes, semideserts, and grasslands that stretch north to the Columbia River and east to the

> *"BLM lands are about superlatives...the largest in the public domain, the least known, the richest in biodiversity—and by far the most varied."*
>
> — DARRELL KNUFFKE, *former Vice President for Field Programs, The Wilderness Society*

Dakotas get a bit more. In the West, noted the writer Wallace Stegner, it is aridity "that leads the grasses to evolve as bunches rather than as turf...that erodes the earth in cliffs and badlands rather than in softened and vegetated slopes, that has shaped the characteristically swift and mobile animals of the dry grasslands and the characteristically nocturnal life of the deserts." In BLM's domain, aridity shapes the arrowy moves of one of the world's largest pronghorn antelope herds in Wyoming's Red Desert and, to the west, in Idaho, the bands of surefooted bighorn sheep in the Owyhee Canyonlands, among the largest of undeveloped areas in the lower 48. In the Colorado Plateau, it bares a unique world of redrock; in California, a remnant grassland that bears witness to bygone American habitats.

If Americans in regions beyond the West have heard of the BLM at all, they usually picture these arid environments. Still, such landscapes only begin to express the amazing variety in BLM's domain that I beheld as I piled thousands of miles on my rental car's odometer. There's a hint of other treasures in the agency's own logo: snowy peaks, winding river, tall evergreen. BLM lands feature them in abundance. This public domain includes some of the continent's highest mountains, looming over mile-high wildflower meadows and abandoned mining camps in Colorado's San Juans. And the long ramparts of Montana's Centennial Mountains. BLM manages 2,000 miles along 36 designated Wild and Scenic Rivers, including six that penetrate deep into the Alaskan hinterland—where BLM administers millions of acres of wetlands, polar deserts, taiga, and lime-white mountains. Oregon's coastal rain forests hold ancient groves of Port Orford cedars, Brewer's spruce, and Douglas fir. To the south, Headwaters Forest Reserve, managed jointly by BLM and the state of California, now protects once-embattled redwoods that were already hundreds of feet tall when the first European explorers saw them. Bruce Cann, of the BLM's Arcata office, points out stripes of blue paint on trunk after massive trunk by a loamy trail, noting that the trees were all set to be logged by Maxxam, the forest's former owner.

Just southwest of Headwaters, in northern California, I hiked along miles of black sand within the 60,000-acre King Range National Conservation Area. Pounded by the Pacific on the one hand, walled off from coastal Highway 1 by peaks of up to 4,000 feet on the other, this "Lost Coast" feels utterly remote even though it's only some 200 miles from San Francisco's northern suburbs. This is wild, rugged country—drenched by as much as 200 inches of rain a year, jolted by frequent earthquakes, churned by rock-slides. Its steepness deterred homesteaders and loggers. Now, splendid isolation has left chunks of undisturbed wilderness, and its 35-mile coast-line remains one of the nation's longest undeveloped stretches.

A more stirring meeting of land and sea is hard to imagine. Congress noted the area's uniqueness in the 1920s, and in 1970 voted to make the King Range BLM's first National Conservation Area—a designation meant to promote management for conservation in places that have special natu-ral or cultural values. Since then, 13 other national conservation areas, 15 new national monuments, and 148 wilderness areas—with dozens more under consideration—have been created, steadily (CONTINUED ON PAGE 38)

FOLLOWING PAGES:

Sandstone-capped escarpment of the Vermilion Cliffs tumbles 3,000 feet to the Grand Canyon in northern Arizona. Vast scale makes the Colorado River's down-cutting appear as a series of narrow, winding incisions near Marble Canyon.

Public lands offer private reveries for paddlers in Alaska's Tangle Lakes area—by morning light, a popular put-in for trips down the Delta River, one of six Wild and Scenic Rivers overseen by BLM in the state.

OPPOSITE:

Denizen of an urban wilderness forages amid the woodlands of Campbell Tract, in Anchorage, Alaska. Moose, along with bear, wolf, and other mammals, make their home in the tract's 730 acres, a natural area popular with outdoor enthusiasts.

FOLLOWING PAGES:

Mojave sundown silhouettes joshua trees in the Virgin River's canyon, south of St. George, Utah.

Cocooned in dust, a ranch
hand and his mount gather
cattle on a BLM grazing
allotment in southern Utah.

FOLLOWING PAGES:
Rugged limestone tors
distinguish the White
Mountains from other
landscapes of interior Alaska.
The million-acre tract, 60
miles north of Fairbanks,
includes just one 15-mile
unpaved road. This is Alaska's
only national recreation area—
and BLM's only one anywhere.

expanding BLM's mission into the realm of conservation. Among them is Nevada's Black Rock Desert, a place as flat as the King Range is steep—home to the world land speed record. These unique places include huge, grand landscapes like Utah's 1.9-million-acre Grand Staircase–Escalante National Monument, a jewel in the Colorado Plateau's crown; millions of acres of wilderness in the California desert; and Arizona's majestic Grand Canyon–Parashant National Monument, which protects the Grand Canyon's watershed. Then again, there's the California Coastal National Monument, a constellation of thousands of tiny Pacific islands, rocks, reefs, and pinnacles that provide important nesting and feeding sites for seabirds and mammals.

"BLM lands are about superlatives," says Darrell Knuffke, former Vice President for Field Programs at The Wilderness Society, an organization seeking to develop a nationwide network of wild, undeveloped lands. "They are the largest in the public domain, the least known, the richest in biodiversity—and by far the most varied."

If all these lands add up to awesome variety, some places stand out for the variety within them. In southern Arizona, the stark and sunburnt landscapes of the 490,000-acre Sonoran Desert National Monument might not at first blush look hospitable to natural diversity. But in fact, those arroyos, peaks, ridges, and grasslands harbor a range of unusual plant communities, along with desert bighorn sheep, mountain lion, rare bats, Harris's hawks, desert tortoise, mule deer, and dozens of reptiles and amphibians.

For natural variety, Cascade–Siskiyou National Monument in southern Oregon is one of the most spectacular spots. It doesn't offer the kind of visual spectacle that starts hearts racing and shutters whirring, as those of the Grand Canyon or Yosemite or even BLM's King Range or Grand

Dusted in snow, the Grand Wash Cliffs sweep toward the Grand Canyon, to the south. Decades of effort to protect the Canyon's watershed yielded Grand Canyon-Parashant National Monument in 2000; the Cliffs are a wilderness area within it.

Staircase do. It doesn't awe by scale; at only 52,900 acres, it's one of the smallest of BLM's new national monuments.

Instead, Cascade–Siskiyou is the crossroads of a 10-million-acre region that is one of the continent's most ecologically diverse. "It's a monument to biodiversity," says forest ecologist Dominick DellaSala, whose employer, the World Wildlife Fund, opened an office in nearby Ashland, Oregon, in 1998 to highlight the region's importance. "Since then, the more I've looked, the more exceptional I've realized it is." He ticks off some figures: 3,500 different kinds of plants, among them rare lilies like the insect-eating cobra lily. The world's most varied conifer forest. At least 110 different butterfly species. "You see that diversity because of the richness in plants," DellaSala adds. "Butterflies are very specialized pollinators." Also, there are 235 different kinds of mollusks, most found nowhere else. "What we have here is a melting pot, a birthing ground for new species."

"These lands that no one wanted have now become priceless. They are some of the harshest, most intriguing landscapes you'll ever see."

— Hugo Tureck, *Montana rancher*

To show me why that's so, DellaSala takes me for a walk along a segment of the Pacific Crest Trail that follows a high ridgeline. Emerging from the trees, we face Pilot Rock, a 400-foot tower of volcanic basalt that guided pioneers on the Applegate-Lassen Trail in the 19th century. To the south, a snowy summit rises from Mount Shasta's perfect cone. We're at the edge of the young, volcanic Cascades; just to our west are the truly ancient Siskiyou and Klamath ranges; the Sierra Nevada has roots here, too. "The recipe for biodiversity is geology plus time plus climate," DellaSala explains. "There's been plenty of time for evolution to start developing new species. And there's a lot of variation in climate." The region also remained an ice-free evolutionary refuge for a great number of plants and animals during past ice ages.

A grand meeting place of geological eras, mountains, soil types, habitats, plants, animals: These canyon-cut slopes and grasslands undulating into the distance are known as a "knot," a rare and important place of natural convergences. Later, I talk with Dave Willis, chairman of the Soda Mountain Wilderness Council, who fought for years to protect the place. This very small national monument, he says, "is a biodiversity bargain because by keeping it intact it benefits a much larger area."

That's not to say that this special place is entirely a primeval Eden. The white firs, shrub oaks, and lichen-draped cedar groves we hike through are young and dense, recolonizing land where many decades of logging and fire suppression have altered natural processes. So have grazing—a traditional activity—and recreational off-road vehicles—an increasingly popular new one, here and elsewhere within these lands. The proclamation that created the monument in June 2000 allows grazing to continue but sharply limits logging and off-road vehicle use.

"The point is not to remove the human footprint, but to minimize it," says DellaSala. At the other end of the spectrum, some feel just as strongly that any limitation on human use is unacceptable and continue to bitterly fight the monument's designation and boundaries.

So it goes with many BLM areas, and especially with some of those now known to be richest in natural or cultural treasures. Traditionally, these public lands have been open to all comers for many sorts of activities, and the vast majority continue to be. But things have been changing in two major ways during the last several years. First, the agency began to focus more on the stewardship of its outstanding natural legacy. And second, the West's growing population now puts almost everyone in the region within a two-hour drive of BLM lands. They are becoming the lands everybody wants to enjoy.

"These lands that no one wanted have now become priceless," says Hugo Tureck, who runs cattle on BLM land in central Montana. "They are some of the harshest, most intriguing landscapes you'll ever see."

"The challenge is going to be maintaining remoteness," says Roger Taylor, the agency's field manager for the Arizona Strip, north of the Grand Canyon—one of the most remote places in the lower 48. Always underfunded and understaffed, the BLM already has to juggle more uses, more people, and more factions than ever. "There are so many more demands now than ever in the past," he adds.

While the BLM slowly evolves, the West itself hurtles headlong into a populous, urbanized future. There, and in Alaska, the public domain represents most of what's left of the wide-open spaces of yesteryear. That in itself gives many of them their highest value. For everything else they have, these lands still offer space enough to expand the spirit. And room enough to get lost. By design. ■

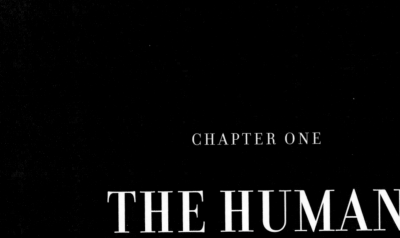

CHAPTER ONE

THE HUMAN IMPRINT

The Great Sage Plain, in southwest Colorado, plays it close to the vest. You see rolling, shrubby vistas and glimpse occasional shadowy hints of distant canyons. Mesa Verde's fabled ridges ride the southeastern horizon. Not too much else comes to light at first glance—and certainly not the stories embedded in the land.

But what you see is really just a coverlet that conceals the densest concentration of archaeological sites in the United States. Spread across 164,000 remote and rugged acres of BLM's Canyons of the Ancients National

Symbol of prosperity, an Ancient Puebloan tower still stands over a village site in Canyons of the Ancients National Monument. The Puebloans' far-flung culture may have stretched the land's limits by 1300, when sites stood deserted.

PRECEDING PAGES:

Land whipped into dust by a dry winter offers little forage for cattle on a Utah BLM allotment; in spring, their owner must drive them to higher, wetter ground.

Monument, the sites represent many millennia of human history. Villages, cliff dwellings, great kivas, shrines, check dams, sweat lodges, croplands, towers, and rock art mark the long tenure of the Ancestral Puebloans, formerly called the Anasazi.

More than a thouand years ago, a flourishing agrarian culture spread across this austere landscape. The Puebloans grew corn, squash, gourds, and beans, and stored their surplus in pottery jars. They discovered new cultivation methods and conserved soil and water. Populations grew.

"There were more people in this county in the 10- and 1100s than there are now," says BLM archaeologist Lou Ann Jacobson, the monument's manager.

It's early one hot, dusty June morning as we walk around thousand-year-old Lowry Pueblo, the masonry remains of a sprawling village and its large round *kivas*, or gathering places. "There was quite a large community here," Jacobson says, "but it's important to think about how interconnected and interdependent things were across the whole landscape."

Far-flung networks of food and water supplies, villages, and communications wove isolated parts into a civilized whole. Elsewhere in the monument, settlements took hold and expanded in the canyons' upper reaches. But at some point, most archaeologists believe, the Ancestral Puebloans pushed their environment too far. As the population grew, people spread into marginal areas. Natural resources became stressed. Poor soils, along with widespread drought in the 1200s, added to the Ancestral Puebloans' woes. By the year 1300, all the pueblos of the Great Sage Plain, along with those of the rest of Colorado's Four Corners area, lay deserted.

Those Ancestral Puebloans were remarkably successful—much more so than most settlers who have tried to make the West bloom in more recent times. But when you listen to stories of 19th- and 20th-century newcomers who staked claims in the region, a similarity—and a lesson—come through: Boundless as they seem, the lands of the West place limits on human endeavor; as rugged as they appear, they're just as fragile; as beautiful as they are, they can be merciless.

The first American citizens to explore the region, Meriwether Lewis and William Clark, expressed some of these contradictions in the spring of 1805 as they plied their pirogues up the Missouri River through rolling grasslands, steep bluffs, and dazzling cliffs in north central Montana. They had

A work in progress to its original inhabitants, thousand-year-old Lowry Pueblo grew with the fortunes of the Ancestral Puebloans. At first a small structure with few rooms, the living space expanded over some 165 years into a 40-room masonry landmark.

FOLLOWING PAGES:

Little changed since Lewis and Clark's day, the Upper Missouri River's Breaks in Montana defied would-be homesteaders. Their loss became a public lands bounty.

already discovered, with disappointment, the dryness of the plains just to the east. This region seemed even less promising for farming: "This Countrey may with propriety I think be termed the Deserts of America," Clark wrote in his journal, "as I do not Conceive any part can ever be Settled, as it is deficient in water, Timber & too steep to be tilled."

Nevertheless, many hardy pioneers did try to settle here. As I paddled that same stretch of the Upper Missouri almost two centuries after Lewis and Clark did, my eye traced the bumpy contours of crumbling foundations, log cabins, even tilting window frames along the banks. Most of the inhabitants, sooner or later, were defeated by drought or hailstorms, by grasshoppers, poor soil, or simply unbearable isolation. Much of the

land wound up in the public domain and is now managed by the BLM.

When Lewis and Clark first beheld it, the Louisiana Purchase of 1803 had just doubled the young nation's size. The Corps of Discovery's expedition, headed by Lewis and Clark, was created by Pres. Thomas Jefferson to explore, describe, and map the vast new patrimony. But the public domain, as concept and controversy, goes back much further. In 1780, the Continental Congress quieted squabbling states by agreeing that unappropriated lands between the Appalachians and the Mississippi River should belong to one and all, "to be disposed of for the common benefit of the United States." Meanwhile, the Land Ordinance of 1785 and the Northwest Ordinance of 1787 set out methods for the survey and orderly sale of public lands.

Still, the nation kept growing through purchase, annexation, cession, and treaty. The United States acquired 1.8 billion acres, in addition to its original public domain east of the Mississippi; huge chunks became new states or giveaways to railroads and other beneficiaries. Most Americans continued to believe in the West as a land of promise for the little man, the yeoman farmer that Thomas Jefferson had idealized.

"I am in favor of settling the wild lands into small parcels so that every poor man may have a home," Abraham Lincoln later declared. In 1862, Congress agreed by passing the Homestead Act, which provided that any adult citizen or head of household could lay claim to 160 acres of the public domain. Earning title to the land seemed easy enough: Homesteaders could either live on the land for six months and then pay $1.25 an acre, or they could live on the land, work it for five consecutive years, and pay only a small filing fee for the title.

It wasn't easy in reality. Homesteaders filed more than 550,000 entries between 1862 and 1882, but little more than a third "proved up" and became private property. The farther west, the harder. Splitting the country from central North Dakota through Texas, the 100th meridian signaled the beginning of aridity—and related problems. Beyond, wrote Wallace Stegner, trouble "had a tendency to materialize in clusters.... If drought and insect plagues did not appear, there was always a chance of cyclones, cloudbursts, hail."

What worked well enough in the rainy East wouldn't in the dry West. That was as clear as a cloudless day in Utah to Maj. John Wesley Powell, the one-armed Civil War veteran who earned his fame by leading the first known expedition down the Colorado River through the Grand Canyon in 1869. As the government's chief western explorer and field scientist, he

Nineteenth-century inscriptions still attest to the fortitude of emigrants who crossed the plains into central Wyoming. Many paused to carve their names near Independence Rock. Ahead lay greater travails: little grass, few buffalo, the Continental Divide.

also published a *Report on the Lands of the Arid Region of the United States* a few years later, in 1878. In it, he explained why the 160-acre homestead was all wrong for the West. Some areas open to homesteading just weren't arable. Among those that were, a 160-acre homestead with irrigation was too much for a single family to manage—80 acres would do much better. For areas without irrigation available, 160 acres were far too little. In those regions, Powell recommended that each family be given 2,560 acres for ranching. He proposed ways to make water available to many more settlers. A visionary before his time, Powell watched his report gather dust.

Powell also reminded his fellow citizens that agriculture wasn't even the original basis for the West's settlement by European Americans. The pick, not the hoe, came first. "In the East the log cabin was the beginning of civilization; in the West, the miner's camp," he observed. By the time the Homestead Act came along, miners had penetrated deep into the public domain. All the major

All hands turn to branding a new addition to the Dugout herd in southeastern Utah. Out of 700 head of cattle, owner Heidi Redd runs about 650 on public land. Many Western ranchers depend heavily on BLM allotments, where grazing fees remain far lower than on state or private lands. At right, Redd herds cattle from BLM's Beef Basin to a Forest Service allotment, where forage is lusher and soil less fragile.

FOLLOWING PAGES:

An errant Dugout dog finds its way back to safety.

discoveries occurred on public land. So did countless others, in places like the Alpine Loop area of Colorado's San Juan Mountains, modern-day BLM land that's strewn with dozens of old mining camps.

When Powell wrote of the West's "stupendous mining enterprises," that industry's supremacy was already written into law—the General Mining Law of 1872. Also called the Hardrock Mining Law, it covers copper, lead, iron, uranium, and other hardrock minerals, as well as gold and silver. To encourage settlement, the law stated that federal lands were "free and open" to mineral exploration, with no permit or lease required. It simply granted a "right to mine"—and also to take possession of 20-acre parcels

overlying each claim. The United States would get no payment or royalty for hardrock treasure extracted from its lands. The law, which still stands, makes mining the preferred use on millions of acres of public land.

Gold, silver, and other hardrock minerals worth some $20 billion were mined from the federal domain in the late 19th century. But the West's other major industry of the time, livestock grazing, had a much broader impact on public lands. Ranching grew exponentially after the Civil War as individual cattlemen began to run their herds on thousands of acres of public land, sometimes clashing violently with sheepherders and homesteaders.

There were three or four million cattle, mainly in Texas, in 1865; by

1886, 26 million cattle and almost as many sheep filled western rangelands. That year, young Theodore Roosevelt rode the drought-puckered high plains and warned that "Overstocking may cause little or no harm for two or three years, but sooner or later there comes a winter which means ruin to the ranches that have too many cattle on them." That very winter, blizzards and brutal cold buried what little grass remained on the range under sheets of ice; hundreds of thousands of cattle perished in the "Big Die-Up."

As president, the conservation-minded Roosevelt carved national parks, wildlife refuges, game preserves, and national forests out of the public domain. But nothing changed on the public rangelands. Herds competed for forage on increasingly trampled and eroded rangeland—some so remote that nowadays it's difficult to imagine the heavy traffic it once bore. East of northern Arizona's Grand Canyon–Parashant National Monument, for example, is an area called Main Street Valley. It is hours from a paved road, but its name was not given in the spirit of playfulness. As Roger Taylor, the BLM regional manager, explains during a visit, "In the 1920s and '3os, there were hundreds of thousands of sheep here, and thousands of cattle. At night, the light from fires and lanterns in all the camps made this look like a Main Street."This whole area," he adds, was "severely overgrazed." Then drought came, dimming the lights of Main Street.

In 1934, as the Great Depression drove beef and lamb prices downward and the Dust Bowl darkened noontime skies with America's topsoil, the Taylor Grazing Act became law. It closed most public lands to new settlement and created grazing districts that eventually totaled 142 million acres. Within them, the new federal Grazing Service would regulate the number of animals that local ranchers could run, with an eye toward long-term improvement of the range's health. Stockmen would also, for the first time, be charged a fee—five cents per cow per month—for the use of public land. They would also pay for grazing permits, renewable at the discretion of the Grazing Service's employees.

But on the ground, the Grazing Service's 60 employees had little authority and even less power to manage the public lands for rangeland restoration or any other purpose. Still, what little power they did wield was too much for some Westerners—and the politicians who represented them. In 1946, an influential group of U.S. senators simply legislated the Grazing Service out of existence by merging it with the old General Land Office to create an entirely new federal agency: the Bureau of Land Management.

No sooner was the BLM called into being than some of these same politicians introduced bills, in 1947 and 1948, to transfer ownership of federal grazing lands to the states. Unsuccessful, they tried again in the 1950s. And they tried again, in the early 1980s: Their constituents, now styling themselves Sagebrush Rebels, declared that the U.S. government was only a temporary caretaker of the federal lands and demanded that Congress sell them off to the states. Congress declined. But the BLM itself, for much of its

Herds competed for forage on trampled and eroded rangeland—some so remote that it's difficult to imagine the heavy traffic it once bore.

existence, usually accommodated the interests of those ranchers, miners, and others who so resented what they considered federal meddling. As critics joked darkly that BLM stood for Bureau of Livestock and Mining, environmentalists began filing, and winning, lawsuits that called attention to the Bureau's indifference to the condition of public lands.

But no law on the books explained just what the BLM's rightful mission was. It was an agency in search of an identity. In 1976, Congress tried to give BLM one when it passed a landmark law called the Federal Land Policy and Management Act—FLPMA in the alphabet-soup argot of Washington, D.C. Sweeping away old land-use laws, FLPMA directed BLM to manage public lands to be "utilized in the combination that will best meet the present and future needs of the American people." In other words, the public domain should be managed for recreation as well as for commerce; for fish and wildlife as well as for livestock. Ecosystems, archaeological treasures, fossils, and scenery should be cared for responsibly. The federal public domain—FLPMA emphasized that it would remain both federal and public—would also be studied thoroughly for inclusion in the nation's wilderness system, as lands designated by the federal government national parkland and national forestland already were.

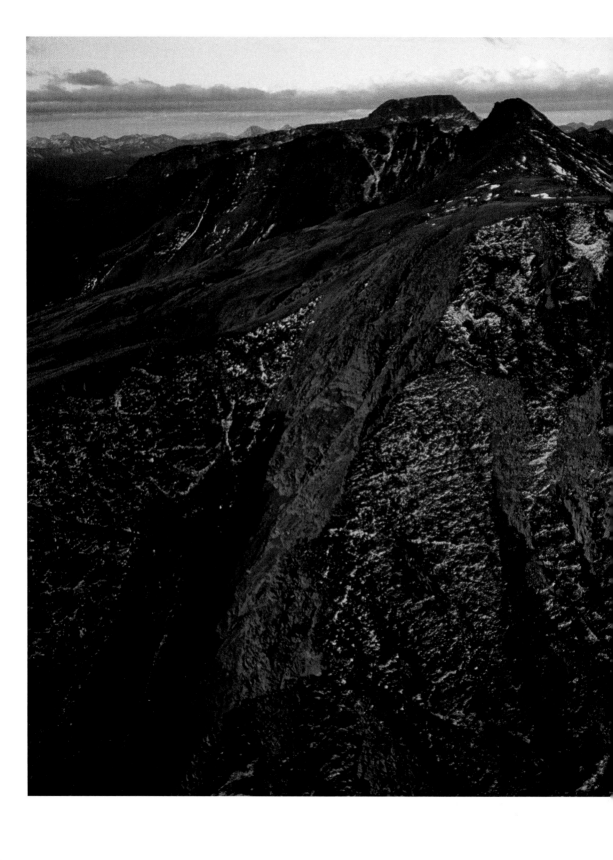

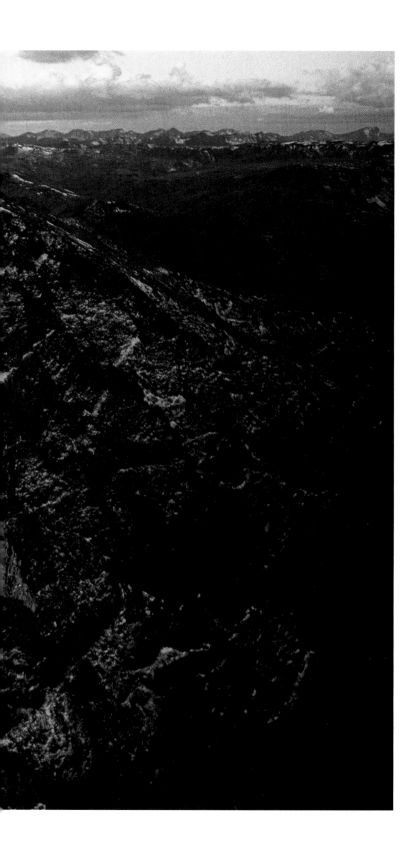

Golden glints streak slopes where miners once toiled for silver, gold, lead, and zinc. Like almost all 1800s hardrock booms, those in Colorado's San Juan mountains occurred on public land.

FOLLOWING PAGES: Mining the federal estate, a dragline moves overburden at Black Thunder, the nation's single largest coal mine—one of many in Wyoming's Powder River Basin.

FLPMA turned 25 the year I went out to explore our nation's public lands. How, I wondered, had things changed in that quarter-century for the ranchers and miners and other commercial users long accustomed to going their own way on the public domain? The answer was usually either "not enough" or "too much." It all depended, of course, upon whom you were asking.

As to ranching on BLM land, there are only a few facts that are generally agreed upon, and many are couched in qualifications. Grazing lands and the streams that run through them are healthier, up to a point. Agency figures show that the improvement that began with the Taylor Grazing Act continued until 1984, but has leveled off since. BLM's field data also show that only one-third of federal grazing lands are even now in good condition. Meanwhile, millions of cows graze on BLM lands. After wrangling in Congress killed proposed increases in the mid-1990s, grazing fees still lag far behind what states charge for grazing on their lands, and BLM's fees are only about one-tenth those that private landowners charge. Half of those fees are returned to ranchers for "range betterment"—fences, water tanks, and the like.

The public domain, including grazing lands, is managed by about 6,000 more BLM employees than there were in 1976, among them wildlife biologists, hydrologists, and range conservationists who deal with grazing issues. Still, most would agree that the agency remains short-staffed and under-budgeted, especially compared to the other land-managing agencies.

"Those busted grazing lands out there reflect a lack of monitoring," says Nevadan Rose Strickland, former chair of the Sierra Club's national grazing committee. "BLM is indeed short-staffed, but there's also not enough accountability, because their people are still rewarded for issuing permits, not for going out and seeing what's happening on the ground."

Not everyone would agree. "There are more and more BLM people regulating me all the time," grumbles fifth-generation Utah rancher and former county commissioner Dell LeFevre, who runs cattle on 190,000 federally owned acres in Garfield County. Since 1996, these allotments have been part of the new BLM-run Grand Staircase–Escalante National Monument. "Some schoolkid's trying to tell me what to do. I don't need a BLM technician; I need a rain gauge."

"The bottom line is that the environmentalists, and the BLM, want us off the land," he continues, saddling a horse for the ride out to a distant pasture. Still, LeFevre would be the first to admit that if he gives up ranching, it won't be because of either group. He is successful by local standards, having bought out 17 other ranchers and acquired their grazing permits. He also owns valuable private ranchland in an area popular with affluent second-home buyers. But the economics of ranching have simply turned against him. "We can blame anyone we want to, but there's just no money in it anymore," he says. Beef prices are stagnant. "In 1973, when I started, you could buy gas for 40 cents a gallon. That's sure changed. But the price of cattle hasn't."

In years to come, there will likely be fewer and fewer Dell LeFevres—individuals who run cattle on public land for a living. Already, their numbers are shrinking. Not only are they going broke, but they are also becoming economically irrelevant, as the national appetite for beef is satisfied by midwestern feedlot operators, who fatten cattle for the slaughter in huge pens. Less than four percent of the nation's beef now comes from rangeland cattle.

"The economics are so unfavorable that the small guys have perished or are perishing," says rangeland scientist Jerry Holechek of New Mexico State University, a grazing expert. "In 20 years, there will still be ranching on public lands," Holechek predicts, "but the ranchers will be even fewer." Across the West, the top tenth of BLM permit holders—often large corporations—controls two-thirds of all livestock on BLM lands; they benefit the most from below-market grazing fees and other subsidies. Wealthy "hobby ranchers" are also beginning to run cattle on chunks of public land.

Why worry at all about a small and dwindling group of mom-and-pop ranchers, then? Some argue that the grazing parcels rented to smaller ranchers are in better shape than those used by the biggest cattle operations. Others point out that in rapidly growing areas, small ranches are important for preserving the open spaces that have always defined the West. "If people can't afford to keep ranching, they'll sell off their private land to developers, and subdivisions will fill up the open space," says Holechek.

Though many would argue that real-life cowboys rode off into a movie-screen sunset long ago, there are a few places, often surprising, where ranching traditions still glue communities together. In New Mexico, for instance, many Spanish-speaking villages trace their history to the 1500s—and their range rights to land grants issued by Spanish governors of the day. Long since taken over by the U.S. government, those lands still help support cash-poor families in tiny towns like Cuba. "People have other little jobs here and there, but everyone depends on livestock," says octogenarian Arpacio Gurulé, who ranches with his sons and daughter.

Without public lands grazing, he says, "most people would go out of business."

An hour's drive from tiny Cuba, New Mexico, the people of Zia Pueblo, near Albuquerque, trace their communal land traditions back even further, to the arrival some 800 years ago of their Puebloan ancestors from the Colorado Plateau and other places to the north. "We used this whole area without any boundaries, and shared it with other pueblos," says tribal administrator Peter Pino, gesturing to the sun-baked slopes around the pueblo. Grazing has been important to the Zia since Spanish times. But colonial rule also marked the beginning of their disenfranchisement.

"By 1890, we were down to 97 people, living on 16,300 acres," says Pino. "Then in the 1940s, some of our forefathers started trying to add more land back to save us." At first going door to door in the pueblo, tribal leaders have now collected enough money to purchase or lease and manage more than 150,000 acres of private and federal grazing areas. At the same time, the pueblo itself is returning from the brink of disappearance.

For the nearly 800 Zia now in the pueblo, grazing isn't a living. It is a means of cultural revival, centering on communal traditions and self-sufficiency. Families tend grazing areas together. No adult can own more than 20 cattle. "We try to spread out the resource to as many people as possible. Twenty cattle per family is the limit," Pino explains. "It doesn't allow anyone to become much wealthier than anyone else.

"We're used to being poor," he adds. All around the Zia, though, other pueblos are choosing something different: exercising their sovereign rights and turning to casinos for income. "We reject casinos," Pino says. "We think gaming is the wrong way to make money. People start demanding their own share of everything. We may be money-poor, but now we have land and cattle, and we've never abandoned the old ways of putting food on the table."

Old ways, like the Zia's, have a tough time in the new West. But old symbols live on—like the crusty prospector. Pickax on his shoulder and golden glint in his eye, he stands for western pluck, independence, and hard work. As such, he is still sometimes cited as a typical miner by proponents of the General Mining Law of 1872, the only public lands law not repealed by FLPMA 25 years ago.

Of the 700 million acres of subsurface minerals owned by the United States, most—like coal, oil, and gas—are leased out, and the BLM collects royalties. Hardrock minerals are the exception. So, in a typical year, when

Children of tradition, Angelina and Marlen Pino, with father Morris, tour Zia Pueblo in northern New Mexico. The Zia manage some 25,000 BLM acres for communal grazing.

FOLLOWING PAGES:

Thin ribbon of humanity flows north along Alaska's Dalton Highway; nearby, the trans-Alaska pipeline carries Prudhoe Bay oil south. North of the Yukon River, BLM land encloses both.

hardrock minerals worth one billion dollars are extracted from federal lands, the miners pay nothing to the BLM in royalties. Prospecting, the argument goes, is risky, costly, and time-consuming enough as it is; the law encourages miners to venture into untrodden backcountry and stake new claims without added financial burdens. But the hardy soul that everyone imagines trudging into the back of beyond is not around much anymore.

To get a peek at his replacement, a good place to start would be the operations along northeastern Nevada's 50-mile-long Carlin Trend. About four million ounces of gold, a third of the nation's annual output, comes from the Trend. From above—from a Cessna cockpit or a windblown ridge—the view of the Carlin operations is breathtaking: Miles of open pits, some more than a thousand feet deep, where multi-story electric shovels and

Above the Arctic Circle, harsh conditions are a magnet for Toolik Field Station researchers—themselves irresistibly attractive to swarms of summertime mosquitoes. Since 1975, this outdoor laboratory on BLM land in the Brooks Range foothills has drawn scientists from at least 25 countries, linking local studies in tundra and freshwater ecology with such global issues as climate change and industrial pollution.

haul trucks as big as houses move around like Tinker Toys. Mountainous heaps where ore and waste rock part ways. Vast networks of roads. Round-the-clock activity. North America's largest gold mine, the Barrick Goldstrike moves more than 400,000 tons of ore-bearing rock a day.

New gold mining technologies demand gargantuan scale, unaffordable to most small companies—much less independent prospectors. In the 1980s, when rising gold prices justified mining low-grade deposits, the new methods came into play. Now most of the gold mined is microscopic, yielding as little as .02 ounce of gold per ton of rock, or one ounce per 50 tons. To extract such small amounts, the companies pile up huge heaps of rock, hundreds of

feet high and often more than a mile in diameter. The heaps are then sprayed with a cyanide solution that picks up specks of gold as it percolates downward. At the bottom, the solution is collected and the gold separated out again.

When mountains of land become molehills of gold, massive amounts of tailings and waste rock are left behind. There can be other, unintended legacies: At the bottom of the leach heaps, impermeable liners meant to contain the cyanide solution occasionally tear. Spills and floods can also release toxic sodium cyanide into nearby streams, groundwater, and soils. Waterfowl and other wildlife have been poisoned by cyanide storage ponds.

Opponents of the new mining techniques question its necessity.

"Ninety-nine percent of all gold ever discovered is still in circulation," says former Secretary of the Interior Bruce Babbitt, who argued unsuccessfully for reform of the Hardrock Law while he was in office. "There's plenty of it around." Moreover, most of the gold now mined goes into jewelry, he points out. "It is not strategically important at all," Babbitt says.

But defenders of the hardrock mining industry say that state-of-the-art environmental technologies are more than a match for the new mining methods. One company that put its money where its mouth is to demon-

Near Lonely, Alaska, caribou pass by a fuel tank at a now unmanned Distant Early Warning (DEW) Line radar station. Drums date back to a campsite for oil and gas exploration, closed in 1983.

strate their point is Homestake, whose McLaughlin operation in northern California mined the state's biggest gold strike in the 20th century. Former environmental manager Raymond Krauss states the challenge simply. "There are two words for someone in my position," he says, "containment and reclamation. None of it is rocket science."

McLaughlin stuck to its pledge to contain the mine's poisons and pollutants. By the time mining ended, on schedule, in 1996, Krauss had been working for years with university researchers, native plant specialists, environmental activists, government officials, and even a local winery, who all helped with the reclamation. When Krauss drove me around the remote, rolling 10,000-acre site, I had a hard time telling nature-made slopes from those shaped by backfill and planted with native grasses. The site itself blended into the nature preserves beyond its boundaries. There were deer and other wildlife; the huge tailings pond was on its way to becoming a wetland.

"Sound environmental management is just good business," says Krauss. Doing things right, he asserts, minimizes delays and legal battles. In that case, I wondered, why don't all hardrock mines take that approach? "If they don't, it's not because they're devious—just dumb," Krauss asserts.

The problems usually don't arise from a lack of rules and regulations—including the Clean Water and Endangered Species Acts and other federal and state laws never dreamed of when the Hardrock Act became law in 1872. Barrick, for instance, obtained about 130 federal, state, and local permits for its Goldstrike mine. "The tools are there to prevent problems, but BLM seldom follows through," says Krauss, who helped advise Congress in 1999 as a member of the National Research Council's Committee on Hardrock Mining on Federal Lands. "We concluded that BLM doesn't have the resources to monitor sites—they couldn't say, for example, how many permit violations there were."

Only once has a permit to mine ever been denied, even though since 1976 FLPMA has required the Bureau of Land Management to prevent "unnecessary or undue degradation" of public lands. Until 2002, BLM required no mining permit for a site smaller than five acres—which covered a great number of mines. In northern Nevada, James Lindsay, a geology student and seasonal BLM employee, told me, "I go into these areas before they start exploration, and some of them are just pristine. Knowing that they're about to get all torn up makes me really sad. But the country does need the minerals."

How long would those mines be productive? In 1999, the companies that owned 36 mining projects in Nevada declared bankruptcy. But when the mines go, their problems sometimes stay behind. About 30 hardrock-mining operations are now EPA Superfund sites, so toxic that the federal government has mandated their cleanup; another 16,000 or so abandoned mines, seriously contaminating groundwater and streams, are not scheduled for cleanups.

At first, when BLM issued a permit to expand a gold mine next to their central Montana ranch in 1988, Stephanie and Alan Shammel weren't concerned. "We thought it would bring jobs to the area, and we heard the new technology was good," Stephanie says. But by the time the Kendall mine shut down in 1995, their ranch and neighboring properties had been polluted by a devil's brew of cyanide, chlorine, arsenic, selenium, and other toxic by-products of the mining operation. Calves, fish, and trees died. To make matters worse, the operation used so much groundwater that springs and streams dried up.

Modern boomtimes are also forging unlikely alliances among Westerners in other parts of the public domain.

Six years after Kendall ceased operations, the cleanup was unfinished and the Shammels' property remained seriously contaminated. The mine's Colorado-based owner, Canyon Resources, refused to foot the entire multi-million-dollar cleanup bill. As the Shammels and other families sued, Canyon Resources announced plans to sell land near the mine site to raise cleanup money—while expanding mining operations elsewhere in Montana.

The Shammels have had plenty of unhappy company in Montana over the years. As gold prices fell in the 1990s, mine names like Kendall and Zortman-Landusky came to symbolize environmental contamination on a grand scale and cleanup price tags in the hundreds of millions of dollars. "There's a consistent pattern, in large and small companies alike, of technical failures whenever cyanide is used," asserts Jim Jensen, executive director of the Montana Environmental Information Center, who drafted a ballot measure to rid the state of it. The Shammels drove 200 miles from their ranch to the state capitol in Helena to testify in favor of the initiative, and in 1998, the citizens of Montana voted to ban most cyanide-leach mining. New federal rules, announced at the end of the Clinton administration, would also, finally, have given the BLM more power and responsibility to prevent damage from the hundreds of hardrock mines it permits. But by the end of 2001, the Bush administration had announced a new, weaker set of standards.

"No one should be allowed to destroy someone else's property—to leave a mess and walk away," says Stephanie Shammel.

"I never thought I'd turn into an environmental activist," she laughs ruefully. Modern boomtimes are also forging unlikely alliances among Westerners in other parts of the public domain. Nowhere is this truer than in Wyoming, a state rich in both ranchlands and energy resources—oil, coal, and natural gas. And in no part of the state is it truer than in the Powder River Basin. Bigger than New Hampshire and Vermont put together, this region stretches from the Bighorn Mountains, in the middle of the state, toward the eastern border and up into southeastern Montana. The massive coal seams that underlie the Basin started its first boom, in the 1970s. Much of the nation's coal today comes from operations that strip-mine federally owned deposits, including Black Thunder, the single largest coal mine in North America.

In the waning years of the 20th century, those deposits launched another, potentially even bigger bonanza as new technologies came online to free natural gas, or methane, attached to the coal beds. Geologists estimate that there may be a year's supply of natural gas for the entire nation in the Basin. In 1990, there were a few dozen coal bed methane wells operating; a decade later, nearly 100 were being drilled each week in the Powder River Basin. By the time supply peaks, say gas companies, there could be as many as 80,000 wells answering the nation's ravenous demand for fossil fuels. More than half would be on federal land leased out to private companies by the BLM.

"Natural gas is a clean, safe, efficient, and reliable fuel," says Kevin Kilstrom of Marathon Oil Company, one of the largest producers in the Basin. "Coal bed methane can be safely developed to help meet the growing energy needs of the U.S.," he says, adding that it will be especially important for new power plants.

Powder River Basin ranchers often see things differently. Their homesteading ancestors usually gained title only to the surface of the land, not what's underneath it—including oil and gas. Nowadays, ranchers have little right to stop whoever does own the underground mineral rights from coming in and installing drilling rigs, pipelines, pumps, overhead power lines, compressor stations, and a spaghetti bowl of roads on their ranches. "People who live on federal minerals have little negotiating power, because

Montanan Stephanie Shammel feeds pet fowl at home. After a gold mine's toxins contaminated her ranch, she talked turkey with state legislators, who banned most cyanide-leach mining.

FOLLOWING PAGES:

Truckers chew each other's dust across Wyoming's Red Desert, where a boom in oil and gas drilling now brings heavy vehicles to roads originally meant for the occasional pickup truck.

in most states, mineral rights dominate surface rights," says organizer Jill Morrison of the Powder River Basin Resource Council, an alliance of ranchers and conservationists fighting to minimize the impact of coal bed methane drilling. "A lot of these situations are like forced marriages, and the landowner is the unhappy spouse."

Ranchers are particularly worried about what's happening to their water supply. Natural gas is held to coal seams by the force of water; to get the gas out, drillers pump water out also—almost 200 million gallons a day at this point. In a region that gets only about 10 inches of rain a year, everyone depends on groundwater. Now, the water level in local aquifers is falling fast, and ranchers say their wells are drying up. Ironically, once pumped to the surface, the excess water often has no place to go—laden

Water everywhere and not a drop
to drink: A sailor's lament
strikes a chord with many
Powder River Basin ranchers,
who find their lands awash in
salty water, pumped from deep
coal bed methane wells. Though
underlying private property, the
wells are often federally owned
and leased to energy companies.
At right, workers tie down chains
on a rotary drilling rig elsewhere in gas-rich Wyoming.

with minerals, it won't serve for irrigation; it can pollute waterways and flood rangeland.

"The companies and the government think everything should've been done yesterday," says rancher and veterinarian Eric Barlow, who is fighting to keep private developers from setting up more than one hundred planned methane wells on his family's 18,000-acre ranch near Gillette. "I think there's a way to do it responsibly, but no one is stopping to consider what's happening. How long will it take for our aquifers to recover? No one knows. And what is it doing to the land itself, and to wildlife habitat? A lot, I think."

"We're learning new things as we go along," says Richard Zander of the BLM office in nearby Buffalo, which hired 25 new employees to work with the industry. "There are valid concerns that we need to address, including water management." The agency temporarily stopped leasing new wells during a basin-wide environmental study—which concluded that intensive development would have profoundly negative consequences. BLM officials in Washington dispute the findings; activists accuse the agency of rushing thousands of wells into production before the study began.

"It's like a gold rush," says Eric Barlow. On the once empty plains of the Powder River Basin, the signs are everywhere, from the sprawling new trailer camps to the 18-wheelers hauling gleaming polyethylene pipe, to the earthmovers and thickets of red flag markers on the treeless hillsides. Roads are clogged, public services stretched. But the strangest thing you notice is how white some of the land looks—and then you realize that it's the spreading layers of salt that rise to the surface with all the pumped water.

"Each well will only produce for 10 or 12 years," says Barlow, "but the effects will be with us for decades or even centuries to come."

As he speaks, most Americans haven't heard of this energy phenomenon. In the West, though, coal bed methane is just one more boomtime player making big footprints in the public domain—no matter how diligently the producers work to erase them. And, like many other things people have done in the West's big dry spaces over time, this energy play is testing the limits of a rough, fragile landscape. Inside the BLM, it's posing a divisive question: how hard to look for high ground in this tricky terrain. ■

For families of Wyoming's vast Wind River Reservation, natural gas means income, with 95 percent of revenues for the Shoshone and Arapahoe who live there coming from conventional gas drilling. BLM helps handle the new leases, but tribal elders may veto sites that hold sacred significance.

CHAPTER TWO

SEAS OF SAGE, ISLANDS OF LIFE

Of all the harsh things ever said about sagebrush, Mark Twain probably said them best. In this "infernal soil nothing but that fag-end of vegetable creation, 'sage-brush,' ventures to grow," he wrote in 1861. He likened it to a "Lilliputian cedar tree" made of the stiffest telegraph wire, its odor a marriage of magnolia and polecat.

It "is the ugliest plant that was ever conceived of," Twain concluded.

Sagebrush may symbolize the West's wide-open spaces, but Twain, like many other sunstruck visitors, would have preferred to see more of the color green. That was the familiar, soothing color of home, of the spreading canopies of shade trees and lawns and leaves. There was nothing like that in the gray, wiry jumbles of vegetation they saw out here

Sagebrush country rolls past volcanic outcroppings in Idaho. Long considered little more than wasteland, the natural environments of the Great Basin in fact offer inviting habitat for mammals ranging from bobcats to pronghorn antelope, along with a multitude of birds, reptiles, and more than a thousand species of insects and other invertebrates.

PREVIOUS PAGES:
Under a rainbow, lands greened by April rains undulate across an Idaho landscape.

in the "big empty." In these arid lands, nature seemed barely alive—unnatural. Except for the mountains: Explorer John C. Frémont wrote in 1848 of the Great Basin, "Sterility...is the absolute characteristic...no wood, no water, no grass."

Frémont was dead wrong. These vast lands between the Rocky Mountains and the Sierra Nevada are home to a

In the wake of a juggernaut, firefighters attack smoldering embers near Clear Creek, Idaho. Elsewhere, the same blaze would burn on for weeks—mostly on Forest Service land—during the infamous summer fire season of 2000. At right, BLM employees in Oregon unleash a prescribed burn to clear out potentially flammable undergrowth .

FOLLOWING PAGES:

A wall of flame snakes up an Idaho ridge. Lightning sparked it—and dozens of other blazes that roared across the bone-dry Great Basin during the summer of 2000.

multitude of animals and plants, exquisitely adapted to extreme heat, cold, and dryness. Sagebrush, for example—actually several different species—unfurls tiny oiled leaves carpeted with hairs that reflect sunlight and slow evaporation. A sturdy root system reaches six feet down and nine feet outward, plumbing the ground for water and nutrients, firmly anchoring the soil against erosion.

Within the sagebrush communities that dominate the West's land-scapes, most travelers also fail to notice the rich understories containing hundreds of native grasses, wildflowers, forbs (non-grassy herbs), and other plants that feed and shelter a huge variety of animals. Underpinning it all is a living crust of earth woven of lichens and mosses. Many of the

Great Basin's plants and animals are found nowhere else in the world.

Today this landscape is the very heart of America's public domain. It includes most of Nevada, Utah's western half, Idaho's southern third, southeastern Oregon, a chunk of Washington, and slivers of California. More than half of it—upwards of 75 million acres—is managed by BLM. And here is what the agency has to say about its present condition: "A large part of the Great Basin lies on the brink of ecological collapse."

I stand on that brink one August day in northern Nevada. I'm trying to see into the future, but my eyes sting and water from the smoke and heat, and

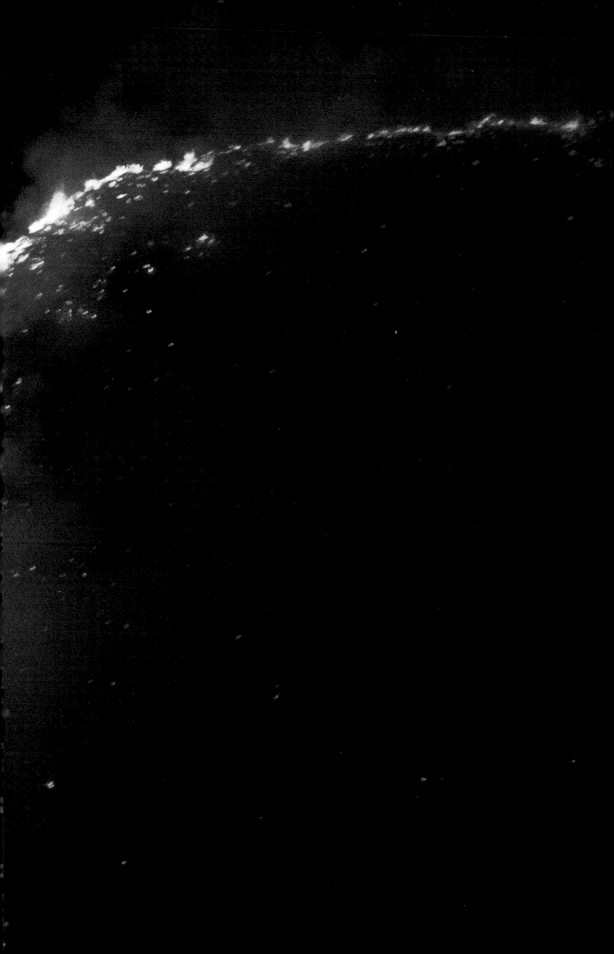

some of the time I can only see a few feet into the distance. What I can make out is charred and blackened rangeland, occasional bursts of flame and lingering smoky palls, the yellow jackets of firefighters working a break. The rotors of a low-hovering helicopter kick up sooty whirlwinds.

Wildfires are both consequence and cause of the Great Basin's ecological condition. But when one starts, and for as long as it rages, there's no time for the big picture—there's only time and room for the picture contained within a specific frame of fire and smoke, in this case the Sheep Fire, a stubborn blaze that lasted ten days, sparked by lightning and powered by big, hot winds. Controlled urgency is the mood at base camp, 25 miles north of Battle Mountain.

"There have been 30 different lightning starts just since yesterday, and the fire's really kicking our butts today," says a weary-looking Nick Zufelt, information officer for the fire. Close to 40,000 acres had burned by this morning. Almost 70,000 by noon. 81,000 now. "These Great Basin fires can grow real quickly with all the grass and flashy fuels." Outside Zufelt's trailer, I can hear the camp meteorologist forecasting shifting winds and isolated thunderstorms as he briefs the nighttime crews about to start their 16-hour shifts.

Four hundred seasonal firefighters have been called in. They rumble into camp in white buses from Utah, Arizona, Mississippi, North Carolina, Alaska, and elsewhere, unload gear, and pitch their pup tents in fields already full of them. Veronica Enriques, Terry Whitemagpie, and the other members of an all-female crew from the San Carlos pueblo near Globe, Arizona, stretch their legs between an 18-hour bus ride and the beginning of the night shift. Krista Kendall, a college student from St. George, Utah, says, "Sometimes you're so tired that you're not sure you can perform, and then you just go forward on lots of adrenaline." Since leaving home less than a week ago, her crew has also spent several days fighting another Nevada wildfire.

For many of those gathering for the night shift, the Sheep Mountain fire, which ultimately burned 84,000 acres, wasn't the first wildfire they fought that summer; most of the crews would go on to fight more big blazes, mostly on BLM and national forest land. During the summer and fall of 2001, more than 1.1 million acres of BLM lands alone went up in flame. The previous year was worse: More than 1.6 million acres of BLM land burned in 2000. And, far worse, in 1999 more than 2.1 million acres of BLM land, mainly in northern Nevada, burned. Catastrophic wildfire is now more the rule than exception of a western summer, says Jack Sept, chief spokesperson for the National

Interagency Fire Center in Boise, Idaho. "We're now seeing fires getting larger quicker, burning hotter, and behaving more dangerously than they used to. It's gotten to be much more of a problem over the last 10 to 15 years." At the same time, growing populations throughout the region put more people and property at risk from wildfire. That in turn makes the expensive and controversial undertaking of wildland firefighting more likely for individual blazes.

Fire is a natural and essential feature of healthy ecosystems. But wildfires are becoming much more frequent—a tightening noose around mil-

---

Fire is a natural and essential feature of healthy ecosystems. But wildfires are becoming much more frequent—a tightening noose around millions of acres.

---

lions of acres, especially in the Great Basin. Before white settlers arrived, fires usually returned to a particular area less than once every 40 years. That began to change around 1900, when an almost indestructible annual plant, cheatgrass, hitchhiked into the West from Asia. By then, heavy livestock grazing had already denuded many areas of their native perennial grasses. Cheatgrass took their place—and took off. As the *Idaho Statesman* noted in 1928, cheatgrass "grows in a day, ripens in a day, and blows away in a day." Sprouting among sagebrush plants, cheatgrass burns so ferociously that firefighters have compared it to gasoline. And since one plant can produce hundreds of seeds, the process begins all over again immediately—eventually burning out slower-growing sagebrush and other natives.

Today, at least 25 million acres of the Great Basin are dominated by cheatgrass, along with other exotic grasses and weeds. And more than 50 million more acres are at risk. Because of cheatgrass, wildfires now occur once every five years, or even more often, in many areas. Each blaze in this accelerating cycle opens more acreage to cheatgrass—a plant generally useless to wildlife or livestock.

Decades ago, conservationist Aldo Leopold called cheatgrass "ecological face powder" that covers the "ruined complexions" of the land. You might also say that the West has more than its share of bleached blonds—lands covered in cheatgrass, an eye-catching, unnatural yellow.

The alien takeover threatens one of BLM's prize properties, the 485,000-acre Snake River Birds of Prey National Conservation Area. Stretching along 81 miles of river and benchlands in southwest Idaho, it was established in 1993 to protect North America's greatest concentration of nesting raptors. The cliffs that soar 800 feet above the river are pocketed with crevices, cracks, and ledges that make ideal nesting habitat for hundreds of pairs of golden eagles, burrowing owls, prairie falcons, and some 20 other birds of prey. Away from the river, 10,000 years' worth of soft, windblown soils are ideal habitat for burrowing animals that raptors eat.

"You're about to get a lesson in pain," says wildlife biologist John Doremus, a little gleefully. In the middle of an open field in the Birds of Prey NCA one morning, he's perched on a ladder, peering into a large nest atop a wooden platform. Three ferruginous hawk chicks peer back at him; nearby, their mother swoops through the air and squawks worriedly, but doesn't approach the nest. Doremus reaches in, retrieving a small downy ball of dark and white feathers with awesomely sharp talons and beak. I'm on. Assigned the delicate task of banding the chick's leg, I fumble along with pliers and metal band, all thumbs, already feeling the pain I know will be inflicted at any second by those talons. But somehow, the hawk forbears—as do its siblings—and soon they're all back in their nest, along with their mother.

Banding and other tracking tools have shown that though ferruginous hawks have become rare through most of their range, they are holding their own fairly well here. Not so with two of the most important birds of prey in the area. Prairie falcons, which nest here in greater numbers than anywhere else in the world, are declining sharply. So too are golden eagles, the biggest raptors in the area. Ask why, and Doremus starts sweeping his arms in all directions.

"When I first came in 1975, everything around here was solid sagebrush," he says. "It started burning a couple of years later, and it's been burning ever since." Since 1980, wildfire has burned most of the National Conservation Area, creating cheatgrass-filled lands that re-burn and expand every three or four years. But jackrabbits, the main prey of golden eagles, need thick, bushy stands of sagebrush for food and cover. Fewer jackrabbits, fewer golden eagles. The same holds true for ground squirrels: When they suffer, so do the prairie falcons that prey on them.

A living tinderbox, downy brome bends in the breeze on California's Carrizo Plain. The Eurasian native colonized the Great Basin, displacing native plants after wildfires. Invading plants "cheated" wheat farmers of crops and bestowed another name on this plant: cheatgrass.

Like Doremus, many BLM employees and other resource managers in this part of the world relate stark before-and-after eyewitness accounts of familiar landscapes. Small wonder, when cheatgrass and other weeds are invading the West's federal lands at the rate of 4,600 acres a day. The stories are legion throughout the Great Basin, and even beyond: In just the past decade, an exotic grass called red brome has invaded Arizona's Sonoran Desert, sparking big wildfires and ravaging the native saguaros and other cactuses of this unique ecosystem.

Today, the before-and-after story involves another disappearing act. BLM botanist Ann DeBolt is along on our field trip hoping to find a rare native plant, slickspot peppergrass. A member of the mustard family, it sports an airy crown of small white flowers, lacy enough to soften the dustiest vista. It grows nowhere else in the world other than a few areas of southwest Idaho. "There used to be thousands around here," DeBolt says as we

In the presence of researchers, a sage grouse anxiously tries to draw them away from her nest of hatchlings at an Idaho field site. A radio collar allows the scientists to track her to her nest, in hopes of uncovering clues to the perilous plight of a species once common throughout the Great Basin's public lands.

hike around a broad upland that seems to have recovered nicely from a five-year-old wildfire. But the invaders may have driven them all out.

"The effects can cascade until we find ourselves at the bottom of the ecological barrel," says BLM ecologist Mike Pellant. What really scares him is a class of newer, even more aggressive weeds—rush-skeletonweed, medusahead rye, and yellow star thistle—that march in after cheatgrass establishes a beachhead. "They're on their way here from the North," he says. "There, some people have already walked away from their ranches because it's too expensive for them to eradicate the weeds."

But he's also optimistic. "We've got a chance to do something while we still have mostly cheatgrass," says Pellant, who coordinates an ambitious and expensive new program called the Great Basin Restoration Initiative. Unveiled by BLM in 2000—in the wake of 1999's wildfires—this new plan aims to proactively consider entire landscapes across the interior West, not simply treat a weed-infested acre here or an eroding fire scar there. Some of its elements, already in use over the years, have been controversial—herbicides to control weeds, or prescribed burning to improve the mix of plants in a particular area. Others, like closing recovering areas to livestock grazing or off-road recreational vehicles, are likely to meet stubborn local resistance. (Both grazing and National Guard maneuvers are allowed within parts of the Birds of Prey National Conservation Area, for example.) Greenstrips—corridors planted with fire-resistant vegetation to protect sagebrush—are already proven to be good buffers; healthy stream banks are natural barriers to weeds and fire.

On 240 acres of BLM rangeland near Boise, there are seeds of hope. Here, at the Orchard Plant Materials Research Site, universities and federal agencies are collaborating to create a microcosm of ecological restoration. After more than a decade of research and experimentation, the area is becoming a healthy-looking spread unlike what you see in much of the Great Basin. Buffered by greenstrips—and protected from grazing and other disturbances—native grasses, forbs, and shrubs, including sagebrush, are competing successfully with cheatgrass. BLM is now buying millions of pounds of expensive native seed for other areas—while trying to interest hard-pressed Western ranchers in growing native plants for seed as lucrative cash crops. But the scope of the problem remains daunting—BLM's "most demanding" challenge, in the agency's own words—and most

High technology helps researcher Nathan Burkepile study a species that adapts poorly to the modern world's encroachments— among them, loss of sagebrush habitat to development. Burkepile's antenna picks up the transmissions of radio-collared sage grouse; his Geographic Information System (GIS) unit pinpoints their location. Below, a day-old chick is radio-collared. At Burkepile's site, hopes focus on hatchlings, who usually don't live past three weeks.

Spikey red penstemons splash color across a shadowy
ravine in Arizona's Aravaipa Canyon. Nearby, buttery
poppies and other spring wildflowers run riot in a sunny
opening in the canyon—a BLM wilderness area where
human access is limited to protect the fragile native flora
and fauna of a rare desert riparian area.

FOLLOWING PAGES:

Horses from a neighboring ranch graze on Aravaipa
Canyon's lush bottomland. BLM attempts to monitor such
threats to native plants.

scientists agree that progress will have to be measured, acre by acre and
dollar by hard-won federal dollar, in decades, if not centuries.

The plight of one flashy-feathered resident could force the issue much
sooner. For mule deer, pronghorn antelopes, jackrabbits, and other animals
whose numbers are falling in the West, a healthy sagebrush habitat is important. For sage grouse, it's the difference between survival and extinction.

Among the largest upland birds in the West, sage grouse are known as
sagebrush obligates—they can't live without it. As Rachel Carson observed
in *Silent Spring*, "The sage and the grouse seem made for each other."
Sagebrush is food, cover, and nesting site to them. And they need plenty of

it. "Birds like pheasants and ruffled grouse might range 10 square miles, but sage grouse range over more than 600 square miles, about the area of Rhode Island," says biologist Jack Connelly, a sage grouse expert who works for the state of Idaho. Connelly says that the birds need variety: exposed sagebrush in the winter; nesting sites with grasses, forbs, and insects in the spring; forbs for food and sagebrush for cover in the summer.

A tall order? There were as many as two million when Lewis and Clark introduced the world to the "cocks of the plains." In ceremonial dances, Native Americans imitated the birds' springtime mating displays, when males fan their brown and white tail feathers into spectacular spiked crowns, puff out

yellow chest sacs strut at dawn, seeking females. In the early decades of the 20th century, "sage chickens" were still so common that hunters bagged them by the dozen for the dinner table. The birds lived throughout sagebrush habitat, in sixteen western states and three Canadian provinces.

But no more. Sage grouse have disappeared from five states and British Columbia; in the rest of their range, their numbers are plummeting—to a total of some 150,000. Like most of his colleagues, Connelly recites from a list of usual suspects: wildfire, development, poor land management, habitat fragmentation... As he does, we're bouncing along on a dirt road in rural southeastern Idaho, and yet even here, he has no trouble pointing out examples of each.

Most of the decline is fairly recent. "Just from 1979 to the mid-1990s, we've seen declines of 80 percent in breeding populations," Connelly says. And the news now coming from Connelly's field sites is even more ominous. That includes the remote BLM land in northeastern Idaho that Connelly and I are heading toward today.

There, we find wildlife graduate student Nathan Burkepile and technician Amy Lewis wandering windswept slopes with a large receiver antenna and headphones, hoping that beeping sounds will lead them to the deeply camouflaged sage grouse chicks they radio-collared as new hatchlings. "We've been trying to monitor them for their first three weeks," says Burkepile, "but their survival has been so low that we're going to need to radio-collar some others."

Connelly expands, "Three out of four chicks are dying before they reach three weeks of age." It's probably not a freak event—the numbers were comparable in the first two years of this four-year project. But as of yet, Connelly can't pinpoint the reasons.

Regardless of cause, the alarming decline of the sage grouse has prompted some conservationists to propose listing it as threatened or endangered. According to Mark Salvo of the American Lands Alliance, an environmental group, "Sage grouse are at about 8 percent of their historic numbers. That's where the spotted owls were when they were listed as a threatened species."

"The next spotted owl?" The question, posed by dozens of headlines across the West, sends shivers down the spines of more than a few federal land managers, ranchers, energy developers, and others who recall the significant land-use changes mandated by the listing of spotted owls by the U.S. Fish and Wildlife Service in 1989. The impact of listing sage grouse in order to bring them back from the brink of extinction could be even greater: Spotted owls live

Herder moves his flock across Oregon's high desert. In the late 19th century, ranchers brought in sheep to browse shrubs on public lands stripped by cattle of native grasses and herbs.

FOLLOWING PAGES:

Airborne wranglers corral a thirsty herd in Eureka, Nevada. Wild horses compete intensely with wildlife and livestock for water and forage.

in the relatively small confines of ancient forests; sage grouse habitat stretches across more than 100 million acres of the West. A listing would probably bring landscape-scale change to BLM lands—from energy-rich Wyoming, where the birds live atop valuable untapped oil and gas deposits, to the vast rangelands where livestock and wild horse herds compete for the same grasses and forbs that sage grouse need for food and nesting.

The sage grouse could become the next spotted owl, but to most ecologists, it's already the canary in the coal mine—a sign of dangerous imbalances across a huge landscape. Colorful and charismatic, the bird is a compelling symbol of its habitat. But it's only one of the sagelands' many native animals and plants that have had trouble adapting to newcomers, whether people or

Prison inmates take the reins of a program at Wyoming Honor Farm, in Riverton, for gentling wild horses captured on BLM land. A public auction, below, follows a three-month program; some auctions lead to dozens of adoptions. Of horse-gentling, lead man David Albaugh says, "Most guys would say it changes you. It's an experience they've never had: They learn that if you give a little, the horse will give back."

livestock or exotic plants. Some of those newcomers, like the wild horses, descendants of the conquistadors' mounts, have themselves now become embattled emblems of the West—cherished symbols of freedom and space to some, weedlike aliens to others.

These lands have always gotten far less attention than the region's forests, mountains, and rivers. Still, "BLM lands are tremendously important to wildlife," says Susan Rieff, director of land stewardship for the National Wildlife Federation and former Department of the Interior official. "Many threatened animals need big chunks of land. As we see habitat diminishing all over the country, we look to big unfragmented landscapes

that are only found on public land." Already, BLM lands in the West and Alaska hold more than 1,400 animal and plant species that are endangered, threatened, or rare.

"BLM is now recognizing that large-scale restoration of these lands needs to happen, and that's great progress," says Rieff. Turning the clock back to a time when its lands and waters were a perfectly pristine habitat isn't likely, possible, or, to many people, even desirable. But as the West's private lands fill up, more and more imperiled species only exist on public lands. As it oversees those lands, the BLM has a growing responsibility to make them once again hospitable to the native animals and plants within them. ▪

Deepening shadows signal the close of a long day for a BLM hand at a Nevada corral for wild horses. Peering over a maze of fencing, his daughter views pens filled with horses trucked in earlier from remote BLM lands. After sorting, they will be sent on to adoptions or refuges in several states.

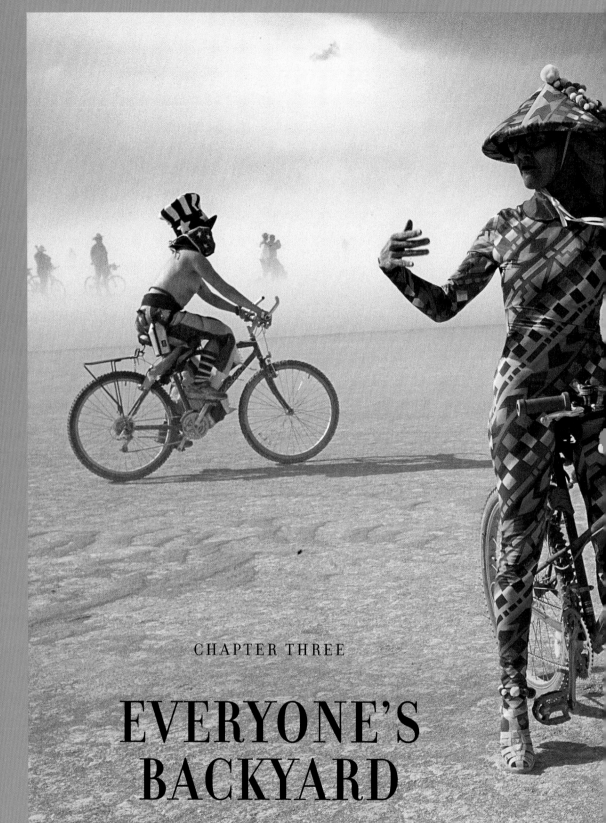

CHAPTER THREE

EVERYONE'S BACKYARD

Not a single vehicle has appeared for hours—not since the pavement ran out past Winnemucca and we set out for the Black Rock Desert, in northwestern Nevada. It's the tail end of a marathon day across BLM land that began almost 400 miles ago in Ely, near the Utah line. Now, chasing daylight and battling boredom, I search the dial for a radio signal, and finally choose the clatter of flying gravel over endless static. After sunset, the stars dazzle, but the rest of the world becomes an opaque, enveloping black. Then comes a noise like a shot. The rental SUV shudders. My companions groan. Flat tire.

As we fumble in the dark with a small mountain of luggage and camping gear and try to make sense of an incomprehensible owner's manual and non-functioning

Answering the call of the wild, visitors to Nevada's Red Rock Canyon National Conservation Area remain within an easy "cell yell" of Las Vegas, a half hour's drive and a world away.

PREVIOUS PAGES:

A wildflower blooms in the Black Rock Desert as California costume designer Jeanne Lauren braves a sandstorm at Burning Man, the weeklong fest in northwestern Nevada's National Conservation area. Beyond, Uncle Sam wheels along the vast playa, one of Earth's flattest spots.

jack, my eye catches a bobbing pinpoint of light in the distance. A half-hour later, moving cross-country, it turns into a shiny white pickup, pulling up onto the road and then stopping ten yards behind my SUV. While my companions wrestle intently with the spare, I walk back to the pickup. The driver, a 40ish, clean-cut type in

A metropolis of mind-bending fun, Black Rock City curves neatly across the playa, laid out with the precision and order of a suburban subdivision. For the week of Burning Man, it becomes one of Nevada's largest cities, attracting tens of thousands of revelers. One of them (below) enjoys a giant, wind-whipped tube.

FOLLOWING PAGES:

Conflagration marks the culmination of Burning Man as the festival's namesake, a 70-foot plywood and neon figure, ignites the night sky during Labor Day weekend.

shorts and sandals, opens his window, asks what's wrong, then leans down to retrieve something.

"See this?" he says, and waves a handgun at me.

I nod and try to hold on to my wits.

"Did you know I'm armed?"

Yes, I nod. I mean no. I mean, I do now.

"You know we all travel armed?"

No. Yes. By now, I can tell this is not some latter-day highwayman lying in wait for the Pony Express or hapless travelers like me. But what does he want? And who is he? Not a rancher, for sure. Doesn't look like a miner, either, or a

rockhound. Who else would be out here? And why is he talking so fast?

"You're in a world of hurt," he spits out three times over.

I agree. Then I suggest that maybe I should go help my companions up ahead. They're struggling with the lug nuts and completely unaware of my predicament.

He nods, but when I start to walk away, he calls me back, shows me the gun again, and nervously goes through the same routine all over again— even faster this time. Then he hops down from his cab to see if he can help with the tire. The gun stays behind, not to be seen again. When the spare's on, he drives off. All's well that ends well.

The tire, though, is shredded. Luckily, one of the two or three places to replace it in Nevada's empty northwest corner happens to be just a few miles away. That's Bruno's Garage, in tiny Gerlach ("Where the Pavement Ends and the West Begins"), which is also the only place in an area bigger than Massachusetts to get a bed for the night—at Bruno's Motel and Country Club. There, over fried eggs and coffee the next morning, friends who've driven up from Reno, a hundred miles south, feast on my story. As locals, or nearly so, they offer a theory: The fellow in the pickup has a methampheta-

---

"I think it's a great tribute to our country that Burning Man can exist. We have the space and the freedom of speech to let it happen."

— COWBOY BOB, *Burning Man organizer*

---

mine lab stashed in BLM backcountry. I'd heard of such goings-on before. Concocting the stuff is a stinky business—not to mention an illegal one—that quickly gives itself away in better-traveled areas. Mr. Pickup's speedy, nervous moves suggested that he'd been sampling his own wares. Whatever he was up to, he must have also been wondering who the heck *I* was wandering around the back of beyond late at night. He wanted to let me know, one way or another, that I was crowding his territory.

Most of what people do in BLM backcountry is perfectly legal. But, legal or not, more activity of all kinds by more people is pushing into increasingly remote parts of the public domain. Since the end of World War II—and the beginnings of the BLM—the West's population has grown from some 17 million people to more than 63 million. The Interior West was already growing faster than any other region by the 1970s, as the Arab oil embargo brought a new emphasis on domestic energy sources and a rush of oil riggers, petroleum geologists, and coal miners to join a widening stream of retirees and other newcomers. Bust followed boom, as usual, but the region's growth has kept outpacing all others' ever since. In the 1990s, eight out of the ten fastest-growing states in the country were in the Interior

West. Fast-growing Alaska has millions of BLM-managed acres as well.

Las Vegas, Nevada, one of the nation's fastest-growing cities, is surrounded by BLM lands. Just 20 miles and a world away from the glitter and neon, Red Rock Canyon National Conservation Area has been called "the Central Park of Las Vegas." A 197,000-acre playground for climbers and hikers and a haven for Mojave Desert animals and plants, Red Rock Canyon now receives a million visitors each year. Beyond Nevada, some of the fastest-growing cities in Oregon, Idaho, Arizona, and Utah—places like Bend, Boise, Tucson, and St. George—also nudge up against public land. More than 22 million people, most of them urbanites, now live within 25 miles of BLM areas. The public domain has become a final frontier, but an accessible one: everyone's backyard.

Even really remote, harsh regions like Black Rock country are feeling the change. Its playa, canyons, and mountains earned a nasty reputation early on. They were "an abomination of desolation" to forty-niners and westering settlers slogging along 120 miles of the Applegate-Lassen Trail that cross Black Rock region. The oxen carcasses that once littered the route are long gone, but wagon ruts and historic inscriptions remain the best-preserved, least disturbed remnants of the West's emigrant trails.

History buffs are only some of the 150,000 people who visit each year now. From yin to yang, cart wheels to jet cars, others come to track 760-mile-an-hour vehicles across the playa—an ancient lake bed that is one of the flattest places in the world. Some come to launch high-altitude rockets and others to land-sail on the playa. Increasing numbers of solitude-seekers head out to the breathtaking canyons and hidden lakes and ten designated wilderness areas in the Black Rock region, which became a National Conservation Area in 2000. Something for everyone.

One day, in the middle of the playa, I see new street signs sprouting from long posts planted in the ground. I walk over and find myself standing at the corner of Oblivion and 6:00. Nearby are 3:30 and Pantaloon and Justice and 2:00, among others. These are intersections like no others on Earth, and it's not just their names. There are, of course, no streets here. No

FOLLOWING PAGES:

Castle Valley's regal monoliths shadow redrock near Moab, Utah. Long shunned for its tortured terrain, the Moab area first found celebrity in 1949, after director John Ford shot *Wagon Master* there. Since then, picture-perfect scenery has provided sets for more than two dozen films.

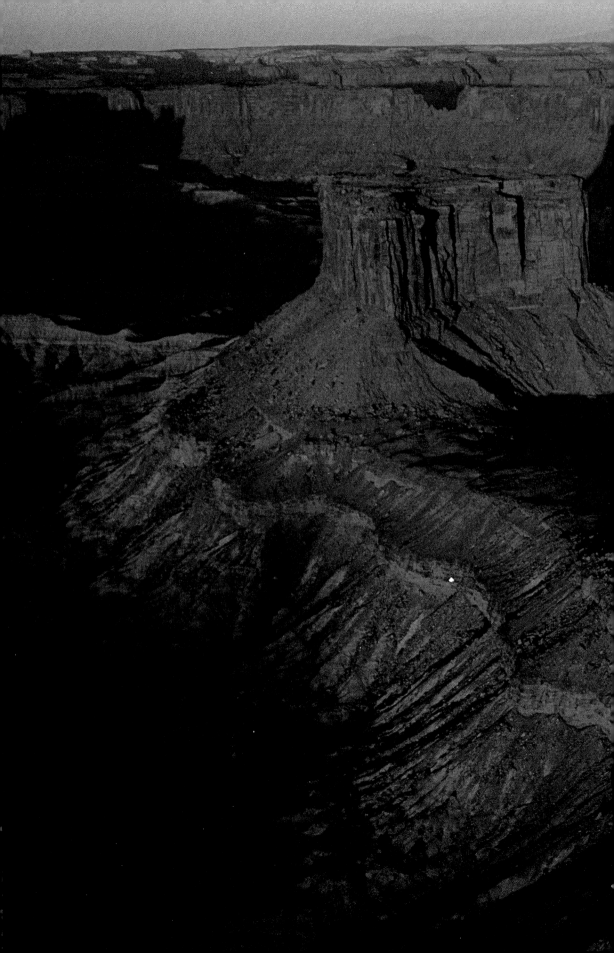

buildings. No city. Only 160,000 acres of perfectly flat and barren desert playa, shimmering hard and white under the indigo sky.

All of that is about to change, though, as it has every year for more than a decade now. Soon, one of Nevada's largest metropolitan areas will briefly take shape right here, when the weeklong artfest and be-in known as Burning Man takes place. This open, empty playa is already becoming Black Rock City.

In the distance I see a shirtless crew from Black Rock City's DPW—Dangerous People Working or Depraved Playa Warriors, depending upon whom you ask—erecting plastic orange fencing that will eventually stretch more than seven miles to enclose the metropolis. Soon there will be an airstrip, a radio station, newspaper, portajohns, a trash recycling station, medical services. Greeters and Rangers will take up their posts. And finally, people from all over the country and several foreign countries will arrive. There will be acres of tents and RVs and theme camps and floats. Costumes that can make those at Mardi Gras look staid. A character called Doctor Megavolt, whose fingers shoot sparks. There will be head-to-toe body paint. Unicycle brigades. Dust storms, art cars, pounding drums, the Purple Dragon, and the Thunder Dome. A ruby red neon heart on a 30-foot mast.

"I think it's a great tribute to our country that Burning Man can exist," says a longtime festival organizer who goes by the name of Cowboy Bob. "We have the space and the freedom of speech to let it happen."

More than 25,000 participants will come this year. Cowboy Bob says they include software developers, doctors, retired military officers, vegetarians, astrophysicists, lawyers, and, to quote him, "rednecks like myself." At the end of the week, everybody gathers to watch the festival's culmination (as if one were needed): the ritual torching of a 70-foot-tall neon-and-plywood man whose fiery demise explodes across the black screen of the desert sky.

Then it's over. And that means *over*: Cowboy Bob says the goal is to leave absolutely nothing behind and begin from scratch the following year. He describes the step-by-step dismantling of Black Rock City. I am fascinated; nowhere else can

Freewheeling four-wheeler flies over the Coral Pink Sand Dunes of southwestern Utah. Part state park, part BLM wilderness-quality land, the dunes are both playground and battleground. ATVers fight for wide-open access; environmentalists for rare plant and animal species.

Bandit-style bandannas shield law abiders from dust on a well-worn trail near Moab. Off-road vehicle riders who stick to BLM's loosely enforced straight-and-narrow are plentiful, but thousands more disregard rules, answering the call of their combustion engines for fresh ground— with growing ecological consequences.

so much over-the-top order and such extreme chaos mingle so happily.

Every year, Black Rock City vanishes, evanescent as tumbleweed. And Black Rock playa is once again a stage empty and big enough to hold the wildest dreams in the West.

They are stages, and artists' canvases, these big public spaces across the West where self-expression takes wing. They are also playgrounds, and refuges, and even churches. In the old West, elbowroom was a creed; in the New West, with so much less of it left, it can be a calling.

There was a time, not very long ago, when the open spaces that captured Americans' imaginations didn't include rough-hewn diamonds like Black Rock country. People thought, instead, of the legendary national parks— Yellowstone, Yosemite, and other crown jewels of the West. A notch or two below the parks were the wilder precincts of the national forests, with their alpine meadows, snow-fed streams, and fir-fringed lakes. Except for the Grand Canyon, Americans didn't often think in terms of the arid lands that, more than any other environment, truly represent the West.

That was all just fine with Edward Abbey—writer, iconoclast, and some-time park ranger in southeastern Utah's canyon country, near Moab. During the 1950s and 60s, Cold War uranium prospecting brought Moab a jolt of prosperity, but when that ended, the area soon fell off the map again. It was, to Abbey, "the least inhabited, least developed, least improved, least civi-lized, most arid, most hostile, most grim bleak barren desolate and savage quarter of the state of Utah—the best part by far."

In *Desert Solitaire* and other works, Abbey wrote with passion and poet-ry about the strange pull of this landscape, of its red canyons and smoke-blue mountains. He also showed readers how to look beyond the vast and grand to the small and the humble—an individual stem of grass framed by sand and rock, or an ancient juniper, "glittering shaggily in the sunrise, ragged roots clutching at the rock on which it feeds, rough dark boughs bedecked with a rash, with a shower of turquoise-colored berries."

If he were around today, Abbey, who died in 1989, would probably regret publicizing this little known land. "Write about something great and here come the people," says his old friend and confederate Ken Sleight, a longtime Colorado River guide. "What it was once can never be again unless you take the people out," says Sleight, who inspired the character of Seldom Seen

Smith in Abbey's novel, *The Monkey Wrench Gang*. The area around Moab—"the most beautiful place on earth" to Abbey—has become a magnet, drawing multitudes to two national parks and two million scenic acres of BLM land.

At first, go-it-aloners steeped in Abbey's writing came for the solitude—for backpacking sojourns amid the naked spires and shady slot canyons; for a trip down the Colorado River, which flows through Moab on its way to Arizona from Colorado—or the Green River, sweeping south in extravagant bowknots.

But what would Ed Abbey have to say about the Cult of Lycra? And who could have predicted that mountain biking would put Moab prominently on the map of the New West in the late 1980s?

Free of gravel and vegetation, tire-gripping slickrock all around the area makes for fine riding. Here in the mountain-biking capital of the world, Main Street is the Slickrock Trail, less than four miles from town. Some 100,000 cyclists a year ride this 10-mile roller-coaster of Navajo sandstone along a high peninsula above the Colorado River canyonlands. Too tame? Time to pedal out to another of Moab's legendary trails—like the Porcupine Rim, where determined uphill slogging deposits you (panting!) at High Anxiety Viewpoint, which juts out over postcard country, 1,500 feet straight down. Then the fun really begins: a 3,000-foot, 10-mile drop down to the Colorado River.

For even scarier thrills, there's Poison Spider Mesa, where you get to fly down a narrow, twisting cliff ledge, dropping 900 feet in about a mile. But for those who slow down, there are other rewards: dinosaur tracks and petroglyphs, undulating slickrock domes to ride over and arches to climb; heart-stopping views of river and redrock, with the LaSal Mountains beyond.

Poison Spider Mesa is also the place to stop for a glimpse of Behind the Rocks, a wonderland of enormous sandstone fins, domes, arches, and cliffs. These days, though, there is something more in the panorama: lots of tire tracks. Thanks to the recent explosion of all-terrain vehicles (ATVs), motorcycles, and other motorized toys, the Moab area is now experiencing a second boom, rivaling mountain biking. At Behind the Rocks, ATVs and motorcycles have wreaked so much havoc that tracts once eligible for congressional designation as wilderness areas no longer are; other Wilderness Study Areas in southern Utah are in danger of the same fate.

Places primeval enough to qualify for wilderness status are officially closed to all kinds of off-road vehicles (ORVs), except on pre-existing trails, according to BLM's own rules. Elsewhere on public land, where sim-

Spinning wheels take the place of wedding bells for bride Heidi Cooper, who drove from Chicago with her fiancé to tie the knot atop Moab's Rim Trail during Easter Jeep Safari. Decades old, the annual off-road jamboree draws hundreds of participants. Climbing ranks high with the non-mechanized crowd: a couple boulders adjacent to the Crack House, near Moab.

FOLLOWING PAGES:

Mountain bikers' Main Street, the Slickrock Trail undulates for 13 miles. Afternoon light burnishes the Navajo sandstone; constant use wears it to the nub.

ilar rules apply, the agency sometimes posts signs asking ORV owners to stay on designated trails. Most off-road buffs are happy to obey, but not all.

BLM's challenges with ORV enthusiasts aren't confined to southern Utah. Every winter, the remote Imperial Sand Dunes Recreation Area, 150 miles east of San Diego, becomes the sand toy capital of the world, a playground for high-performance "quads," agile dirt bikes, $60,000 sand buggies, and more mundane jeeps and trucks. The long Thanksgiving weekend kicks off the season, as nearly 200,000 visitors turn the sweeping dunes into a combination racetrack and party pit.

"It's unlike anything else in the world," says the BLM's Thomas

Sharkey, assistant dunes manager for the area. "People come from all over the country to this place that's hours from anywhere, where there's nothing, and suddenly they double the county's population. Then they ride the dunes and party for five days." Unfortunately, that's not all that happened over the 2001 Thanksgiving weekend. "One person died when an ATV quad hit a truck, another from a rollover, and someone fell off an ATV," Sharkey relates. "There was also a fatal shooting." Beer cans and fists flew along with sand; there were hundreds of arrests and citations. A participant called the dunes "the most illegal place in the world."

Throughout the West, sheer numbers are turning ORVs into the BLM's

single biggest headache. And with 2,000 more being sold every day in the United States, these machines, especially the four-wheel all-terrain vehicles, are likely to become a perpetual migraine. ORVs are also becoming increasingly powerful, bulked up with big engines and knobby tires that can go just about anywhere. Up a dry waterfall, for instance, according to one 1999 article in *Four Wheeler Magazine* that described a southern Utah route its author had pioneered.

"No one foresaw the explosion in off-road vehicle use," says Katie Stevens of the BLM's Moab office, which covers some two million acres. But that's only part of what keeps someone in her position busy. Not just for off-roaders and mountain bikers, the Moab area these days is also a Mecca for campers, boaters, backpackers, hikers, climbers, horseback riders—and, most recently, thrill-seeking jumpers who strap on parachutes and leap from cliff tops and pinnacles.

Stevens and I are spending a day touring the Colorado Riverway northeast of town—a mere sliver of her territory. From a gravel beach, we watch rafts full of wet, happy vacationers bob past on a lively current. This is Utah's most popular river trip, the Colorado Daily—a name that almost sounds like a suburban commuter route. Stevens points across the far bank and up a high tumble of redrock. Everything on that side of the river is Arches National Park, though it looks no different from the surrounding BLM lands. Neither, for that matter, does Canyonlands National Park, south of Moab, look much different than the BLM lands that adjoin it. In fact, almost all the area was originally nominated for national monument status. Eventually, only the two smaller chunks, Arches and Canyonlands, made the cut, and later became national parks.

These lands may resemble each other, but the sibling agencies that run them treat them and their visitors quite differently. "The Park Service," one BLM employee who wished to stay nameless told me, "builds a road into the middle of the place, and tries to keep people around the Visitors Center or in developed campgrounds." The Park Service's mandate, for conservation as well as recreation, sometimes means putting fragile backcountry areas off-limits. BLM, on the other hand, has always placed far fewer restrictions on its visitors. "On BLM lands, you've got National Park quality with fewer people and a lot more freedom," he says.

Possibly too much, he and others are beginning to think. "What's so attractive about BLM is that you can come and be absorbed into the landscape,"

Campers and canine soak off springtime heat at Indian Creek Canyon, south of Moab. A magnet for climbers, the area is famous for its climbing routes, especially slit-like "cracks." But the canyon hosts few of the crowds that nearby Canyonlands National Park receives.

Stevens adds. "But with two million people a year, you do need some controls. And those controls take some getting used to"—especially considering BLM's anything-goes reputation, known to Westerners if not visitors from elsewhere.

If anyone could persuade Moab's on-the-move masses to stick to the trail, it might be Jayne Belnap. A world-famous ecologist with the U.S. Geological Survey, she is known locally as Dr. Dirt. And with good reason: No one knows more than she does about biological soil crusts, the living skin that holds arid land together just as human skin, our largest organ, keeps our bodies intact—and protects us from injury as our first, best line of defense.

Few things delight Belnap more than a little show-and-tell on her chosen subject. Just outside her door, it's only a few steps to BLM land that rolls a mile or so to the rim of Millcreek Canyon, its sloping walls fired in desert pastels in the late afternoon sun.

If you thought dirt is dirt is dirt, you wouldn't after a chat with the exuberant Belnap. The descendant of early Utah pioneers, she says that "most ecologists study eastern forests and not western deserts." Thus, among other things, few people know that in the world's dry regions, most open spaces are covered in woven mats of bacteria, algae, lichens, mosses, and fungi. "All these little danglies glue small soil particles together to make a crust," she explains. Once formed, the crusts stabilize soil, prevent erosion, transfer nutrients to plants, and hold water in the ground. They play a major role in many of the earth's ecosystems, a fact just coming to light now through the work of Belnap and a few other scientists.

Even her way of walking through this burnished country hints at a different relationship than most of us have with it. Belnap almost skips. Light on her legs and light on the land, she moves along purposefully but stops to inhale a noseful of sand verbena, then bobs and weaves her way past rabbit-brush and comes to rest, briefly, by a patch of biological crust, dark brown and bumpy.

Belnap is not impressed by it. "Better than nothing," she mutters, looking closely. She points out layers of blown sand all around—the result of a constant low-level sand storm throughout the region, churned up by more and more tire tracks going everywhere, she says. "Sand is very bad juju if you're a crust." In other words, sand suffocates crusts, killing them slowly but surely.

Trampling, on the other hand, destroys them outright. Tire tracks also do that job most efficiently. But historically, hoofprints have done more, and more widespread, harm—right here, for instance, in Belnap's BLM backyard, long open to public lands grazing. "These ecosystems just didn't evolve with cattle, any more than they evolved with ATVs and ORVs pounding them," she says.

I had thought, before we met, that these living crusts would be common, reflecting the natural state of things in arid climates. Not so. Spotty, isolated patches are more the rule—and so are naked, exposed, vulnerable soils, throughout the arid West. The living crusts can only grow and heal when they're wet—which means rarely. "This environment is more fragile than any place I've ever been, and I've been all over the world," Belnap says.

It's twilight by the time we reach the upper slopes of Millcreek Canyon, whose steep areas remain undisturbed by hooves or tire tracks. There, Belnap finally spots something that really excites her: huge clumps of healthy crusts, chock-full of so much microscopic life that their fudge-like color is streaked with pink and yellow, like something left behind by a UFO.

"Oh, the crusties are so nice!" Belnap sings out, and thrusts her hands high in the air in a little dance. "Touch them!" They are furry and rich with moss, and incredibly hard.

Left alone, this is a changeless environment, where life takes its time. And so does death. It's the kind of place where, a ways off, a gnarled juniper has been lying dead—and unchanged—for centuries.

"This is a landscape that time forgot, a very slow, static place," Belnap says. But not anymore. "Now, we need to know how much the ecosystem can take, because the implications are staggering."

Her hands, high overhead a minute ago, come down to shoulder level, and open outward, palms up: An unanswered question. "Maybe we'll begin to know in 50 years."

In one sense, 50 years doesn't seem like a long time for southeastern Utah's public lands. After all, nowhere else is there so much time, and so many different ways of marking it, on such bold display as here. There is, to start, the pageant of geological time in the 300-million-year-old layer cake of cliffs, canyons, and other rock forms. Then, there are the cryptobiotic crusts and ancient junipers, the reptiles lying inert in the afternoon sun, and other living things of biological time—slowed over millions of years into metabolic synchronicity with the rhythms of their austere environment. Finally, there is human time—time enough for the civilizing instinct to gain its foothold in North America, right here in the canyon country of the Colorado Plateau.

How much time? Perhaps a millennium, from start to finish, from the 3rd or 4th century after Christ to the end of the 13th century. And time enough, since then, for all of the cliff dwellings, campfire remains, kivas, pottery sherds, irrigation ditches, and roads that they left all over the landscape to deepen the mystery of the Ancestral Puebloans' fate. There is more rock art—more painted pictographs and etched petroglyphs—in 500 square miles of BLM land in southeastern Utah than anywhere else in the country.

Compared to all these pulse beats on the land, 50 years sounds like nothing. On the other hand, maybe it's something huge. That's because human time here is now measurable by an ever quickening and louder tempo.

South of Moab, hard by the Four Corners, I see what a few hours of fun can do to a thousand-year-old site. This site litters a remote hillside in San

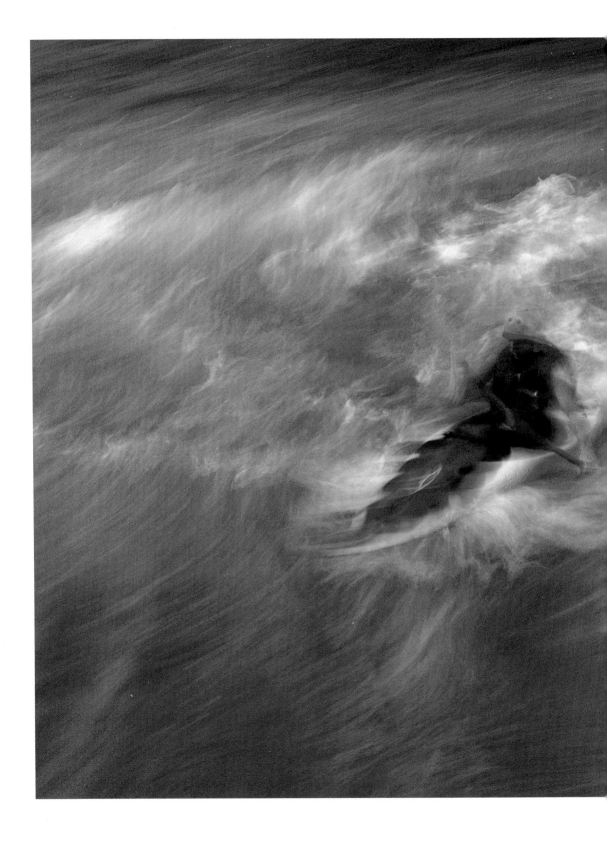

Cresting whitewater envelops a kayaker in the "Mine Wave," one of many white-knuckle rapids on Oregon's Rogue River. Since 1968, BLM has managed a stretch of the Rogue as part of its 2,000-mile National Wild and Scenic Rivers system.

Toasting triumph over the rapids, Rogue rafters join some
100,000 other day trippers who paddle, float, or kayak
the river each year. Nightfall brings tranquility; only a few
lucky winners of BLM's annual lottery can continue into
the Wild and Scenic portion as it rushes toward the Pacific
Ocean near Gold Beach, Oregon.

FOLLOWING PAGES:

Peaks of the Alaska Range rise beyond the Maclaren River.
Farther east along the Denali Highway, boaters put in at
Tangl Lakes for trips on BLM's Wild and Scenic Delta River.

Juan County and is part of the larger archaeologically rich area known as
Butler Wash. Once abandoned, it remained undisturbed until the end of the
20th century.

Then it was discovered by local ATV buffs and dirt bikers, who enjoyed
its open, sandy slopes, and shrugged off damage to its artifacts. Legally,
they claimed, the area was open to off-road vehicles, and in any case, it was
too late to protect the artifacts. As Jim Bourne, head of the Southeast Utah
Land Users, Inc., a local off-road group, commented, "This area was
already 'marked up' by vehicular tracks. Why force them to go somewhere
else?" Others countered that BLM is charged with protecting archaeologi-

cal sites on public land. Attempting to straddle the issue, the agency fenced off the hundred acres deemed most sensitive among Butler Wash's 32,000 acres and left the rest wide open for off-roaders. Says attorney Herb McHarg of the Southern Utah Wilderness Alliance, "They targeted a small part of it as ground zero, and invited everyone to come play all around it."

On a quiet weekday afternoon, Joe Pachak, a local archaeologist, lends his keen professional eye to this "all around" part—still an official off-road playground. Most of the artifacts we see on this slope are Pueblo II, he says, about a thousand years old, though there are hints in black pigments we see of a human presence going back 2,000 years. He shows me several room blocks, collapsed

forms of masonry and mud, where people lived. He points out a midden, bisected by a tire track. On the ground, artifacts are scattered everywhere. Here is a cobble; there, a flake. Joe's friend Vaughn Hadenfeldt, a local archaeology guide, picks up and holds a perfectly round, smooth, white, stone bead in the palm of his hand; hundreds more would easily fit there side by side.

Mostly, we find pottery sherds—too many to count. I pick up a bit of white ware, adorned in slender chevrons with a yucca fiber brush—and a steady hand. Bold red and black stripes alternate on pieces of red ware nearby. Some sherds appear woven. A sample of corrugated gray ware catches Pachak's eye, and he traces the pinched coils that spiral tightly, around and upward, with his fingertips. "Very sophisticated." He shakes his head slowly. "The people who made this knew what they were doing."

The tire tracks produce some patterns too—cross-hatching, circles, parallels—and go every which way. Interestingly, there are also quite a few within the off-limits enclosure. The fence around it apparently isn't much of a barrier.

Scott Berkenfield, who came to the local BLM field office after the enclosure was set aside, says, "Preserving archaeological sites is much easier said than done." It is a challenge in his two-million-acre territory, where new sites are discovered every week. As to Butler Wash, "Some are saying we should close it on an emergency basis to off-road vehicles. But every time we do something like that, we wind up in court."

"It's a common scenario," Vaughn Hadenfeldt replies. "BLM has never had enough money, people, or political will. And now everyone's converging on the agency from all directions."

As more people converge on the agency—and its once-remote lands— protecting a spectacular trove of fossils in its care is also a growing challenge for BLM. A few weeks after my Utah sojourn, I spend a day with BLM paleontologist Laurie Bryant in southwestern Wyoming. Among many things that have kept her working late recently, she tells me, is the discovery of fossil primate skeletons in an area where people want to create a dirt bike playground. A resolution seems far away, beyond the horizon, where a herd of wild horses stands etched against fast-moving clouds.

"You wouldn't think the urban interface would be an issue here," she says. As she speaks, we're an hour from even the tiniest town. "But we're only a few hours from Salt Lake City, and an amazing number of people congregate here for motorcycle racing. We also get lots of rock hounds and many others who love to spend time here." Everyone demands access.

Bryant calls this a "very Zen" vista: "Nothing to see but open space." This is also a paleontologist's paradise, as it happens. "Often BLM got left-over lands that were too hard to homestead, but they're the best place to find fossils," Bryant explains. "No trees, no soil. You can see bare rock all around. If it were warmer and wetter here, that would slow erosion, but erosion is what reveals fossils."

Once it was much wetter and warmer, though. Bryant tells me this was

---

"BLM has never had enough money, people, or political will. And now everyone's converging on the agency from all directions."

— Vaughn Hadenfeldt, *archaeology guide*

---

all a vast tropical lake 50 million years ago, filled with fish, crocodiles, and turtles. Boa constrictors slithered along its banks, while tapirs and tiny horses scampered through the jungly tangle and palm fronds rustled over-head. From time to time, the lake environment turned toxic for the fish, which died in great numbers. Fine sediments buried them in some kind of oxygen-free environment that preserved them superbly.

Now it's about 50 million years later. In a shallow canyon, schools of fossil fish swim by me in a choppy beige sea that runs for many miles along a narrow band of exposed rock. "They look like they were just fished yesterday," marvels Dale Hanson, another BLM paleontologist traveling with us. For scientists, exploring a place like this is like peering into a primordial aquarium. But the delicate, detailed fossil fish are also prized enough to support an outlaw trade that reaches to Europe and Asia. Thieves lift the shale layers that hold the fossils out of the rock matrix using screwdrivers, shovels, or even front-end loaders. Today, the paleontologists notice a few fresh gouges.

All in all, though, illegal activity is down over the last few years, they say—ever since BLM agents caught a few fossil thieves red-handed out here in the middle of the night and a judge handed them hefty prison sentences.

Other fossil looters took notice. But BLM, its belt tightened nowadays, no longer leases aircraft to monitor these sites and instead must depend on a handful of rangers to patrol 18 million acres in Wyoming alone. "The thieves filter back," says Bryant, "because we can't keep enough of a presence here." Or elsewhere in its vast, fossil-rich domain, for that matter. Just two weeks after I met Bryant, BLM announced the theft from Utah of one of world's most complete *Allosaurus* skeletons.

Paleontologists call it a day as night falls over Utah's Kaiparowits Plateau, one of the world's most important study sites of the late Cretaceous era, the end of the age of dinosaurs. With more visitors to its fossil-rich lands, the BLM worries about looting. Dealers illegally sell fossil fish, below, at home and abroad.

FOLLOWING PAGES:
Family tradition of surf casting passes to a new generation on California's Lost Coast.

It's not just thieves. "Fossil fishing," an old family tradition on public lands, was an innocent pastime until it came to the attention of the BLM. The agency itself still contributes to confusion by allowing the collection of a broad assortment of fossils—just about everything except vertebrates.

That kind of relaxed attitude has long distinguished the BLM from agencies like the National Park Service. Nowadays, though, this attitude is

sometimes recast as flexibility—which can be a plus in coping with changing demands in the new West. After the U.S. Army decommissioned Fort Ord, on California's Monterey Peninsula, BLM in 1996 won out against several other government agencies vying to manage thousands of undeveloped acres on the populous central coast. Why BLM? Sheep grazing, among other reasons. It was a Fort Ord tradition that neighboring communities wanted to see continue. Other federal agencies wouldn't go for it. BLM would. Its own habitat experts, working with local groups, now use grazing to keep tinder down and—since sheep prefer non-native plants—as an experiment to get rid of exotic plants and reestablish some of the area's 45 rare natives.

Places like Fort Ord—the largest open oceanfront space, and one of the last, south of San Francisco—can be a haven and a gift for millions of people. Sometimes, though, despite BLM's good intentions, the haven within and the clamoring crowd just beyond fall out of balance. In southern Arizona, the San Pedro River has the poignant distinction of being the last of the Southwest's once common natural rivers—neither dammed, diverted, nor straitjacketed in concrete. As one of the nation's most important riparian areas, it hosts, at least part of the year, nearly 400 kinds of birds, numbering millions of individuals, along with more mammals than anywhere else outside the tropics and dozens of reptiles and amphibians.

In 1988, nearly a third of the river's 150-mile course, and tens of thousands of acres flanking it, became the San Pedro Riparian National Conservation Area. The BLM pulled livestock off the river; sand and gravel mining ceased, too. Within a year or two, sweet clover and ambrosia, young cottonwoods, and lacy willows were coming in thick along the banks. Rare green kingfishers, willow flycatchers, and yellow-billed cuckoos flitted in the trees. Numbers of more common birds like sparrows, tanagers, and warblers soared.

You might be tempted to call the San Pedro an oasis of life in the Sonoran Desert. That would still be partly true, but also ironic, because the San Pedro is slowly being sucked dry. Along with songbirds, snowbirds have been flocking to the burgeoning town of Sierra Vista, near the river. The Army's nearby Fort Huachuca drinks up even more water out of the shared aquifer. On the San Pedro, once lush riverbanks are parched.

"The rivers of the West have almost all been pumped dry or diverted," says Robin Silver of the Southwest Center for Biological Diversity, also a local

Cottonwoods grow along Arizona's San Pedro River corridor, home to some 400 bird species and the greatest diversity of vertebrates in the interior United States. But competing demands for water from growing towns and nearby Fort Huachuca threaten its rare riparian ecosystem.

property owner and an emergency room physician. "I'm just trying to save one that's dying." In this case, he believes the patient can only be expected to grow sicker, as municipal water use continues to soar around the San Pedro.

Antique water rights will have to be untangled, most likely in a court-room, say Silver and others. Here and throughout the West, water law has historically favored agriculture. But agriculture will be a metaphorical drop in the bucket compared to future human water use, which, in Arizona alone, is expected to double within 50 years. In the long shadow of these two play-ers, agriculture and people, will there also be a future for the San Pedro and other special public lands as havens of nature? Once, the booming land-scape around the San Pedro was best known for the O.K. Corral. Chief Geronimo was the headline-maker and Wyatt Earp was the law. But this is not your great-grandfather's West, and these are not the old showdowns. Not by a long shot. ■

Boater Rich Newton clears his canoe after an outing on Alaska's Tangle Lakes; his dog, George, awaits a cue. Most of BLM's vast, remote holdings in Alaska defy easy access. But visitors to recreation areas located near highways, like the Tangle Lakes, also often find themselves alone.

CHAPTER FOUR

MONUMENTAL VISIONS

I n a land touched by wizardry, water is flowing magic.

Through this thousand-mile labyrinth of interlacing gorges, the Escalante Canyons, it travels in glinting filaments, pausing in pools that cup the sky. It drips from seeps in honeycombed cliffs. It can spring suddenly out of the ground, and disappear just as quickly. In this desert world of south central Utah, water is usually as elusive as it is alluring.

Not always, though. High above me one hot June morning, Upper Calf Creek Falls slides off a sandstone ledge and clatters into a cold, deep pool almost 90 feet

Crossbeds of Navajo sandstone paint the Coyote Buttes in hues created by the precipitation of oxides. From a 3,000-foot-high escarpment to a canyon 2,500 feet deep, Arizona's Vermilion Cliffs National Monument encloses a host of geological wonders.

PREVIOUS PAGES:

Oldest conservation area, King Range faces one of the newest components of BLM's Clinton-era conservation initiatives, the offshore California Coastal National Monument.

below. After my hike over sandstone and lava, the falls could be a curtain of moonbeams, framed by electric green mosses and redrock walls, ringed by willows and oaks. Like so much else here, though, it is a fleeting vision. Soon enough, the water that conjures this lushness returns to the world of naked rock and a landscape renowned for harshness. It is one of many tiny tributaries of the Escalante—the last river added to the map of the lower 48.

This "unknown, unnamed river," wrote discoverer A. H. Thompson— John Wesley Powell's brother-in-law and a member of Powell's 1872 expedition—"soon became lost in the multitude of chasms before us." He called it Potato Creek but later renamed it for Father Silvestre Velez de Escalante, the intrepid Spanish explorer who glimpsed the region in 1776. Like Thompson, he never penetrated it. "No animal without wings could cross the deep gulches in the sandstone basin at our feet," Thompson noted.

You could still say much the same thing about the Escalante Canyons, one of three regions making up the 1.9-million-acre Grand Staircase–Escalante National Monument; the vast Kaiparowits Plateau and the Grand Staircase cliffs to the southwest are even more rugged. Death Hollow, Devils Garden, Carcass Canyon, Last Chance Gulch, Harvey's Fear, The Scorpion, Burning Hills: Scattered place names, many given by Mormon pioneers, hint at harrowing stories. There was also a place named Thorny Pasture—until a 1947 *National Geographic* expedition, "The First Motor Sortie into Escalante Land," equipped with 3 jeeps, 2 trucks, and 35 horses, began calling it Kodachrome Flat, so impressive were its multihued rock formations. Much more recently, *Car and Driver* magazine conducted a survey to find the most remote place in the continental U.S., and gave the prize to this part of southern Utah. To this day, no paved roads traverse the national monument.

In the 21st century, it is almost impossible to imagine a place that remains so big and so wild. Beginning near the Arizona border, the 100-mile-long ramparts of the Grand Staircase step northward for 150 miles and upward for 3,500 feet from the Grand Canyon's rim in a series of technicolor risers—the Chocolate, Vermilion, White, Gray, and Pink Cliffs—that put 250 million years of geological history on display. To the northeast, the Kaiparowits Plateau—bigger than all of Utah's national parks combined— holds perhaps the richest treasure chest in the world from the age of dinosaurs. There, paleontologists are turning up fossils of ostrich-like dinosaurs, duckbilled and horned dinosaurs, two-ton meat eaters. And

Gossamer blossoms of farewell-to-spring flutter on slopes of the Carrizo Plain National Monument, where wildflowers flourish amid remnants of California's original grasslands.

FOLLOWING PAGES:

Covered in October snowfall, peaks of the San Juans shear through early morning fog. BLM's Colorado holdings include 97,000 alpine acres, including large tracts of wilderness-quality land.

more: fossil turtles, crocodiles, mammals, birds, trees, flowering plants, and flying reptiles, all of them living and dying in a hotbed of evolution. Nowhere else is 30 million years of life on Earth better preserved—so undisturbed, say scientists who have worked on the Kaiparowits Plateau, that they sense that they're just beginning to scratch its surface.

In every way, this land dwarfs you and cuts you down to fairy-tale size. Staring at the White Cliffs, you're a Lilliputian struggling to scale a stairway chiseled for gods. In the foot-wide slot canyons of the Escalante River, you're lost in the folds of a giant's garment. On the knife-edge of the Straight Cliffs, you ride a stegosaurus's leathery spine. Elsewhere on the 800,000-acre Kaiparowits, the Burning Hills, seething with underground coal fires for hundreds of years, are the rust-red belly of a fire-breathing monster. There are

streams so cursed by alkali and arsenic that nothing will grow around them. But the Kaiparowits also holds a climax forest of thousand-year-old junipers and piñons. And that's just what we know: There are still places amid the arches, mesas, badlands, hoodoos, and canyons that no one has seen at least since their original inhabitants abandoned the area in the 13th century—leaving hundreds of recorded archaeological sites and many more still undiscovered. "There is a real sense of discovery here," says Kate Cannon, the monument's manager at the time of my visit in 2001. "You can still feel like an explorer."

Meandering from the high San Juans to southwestern Colorado's sandstone canyons, the fragile, wildlife-rich San Miguel River corridor enjoys special environmental designations from BLM.

Always, this land reminds you of your puniness in the big picture. But the big picture is what counts. It's what gives scientists an unbroken panorama on the past; it gives elk, bald eagles, and hundreds of other animals the room they need. It buffers many plants found nowhere else on earth from aggressive exotic invaders. As for humans, this place that makes us feel so small physically also has a way of leaving us—some of us anyway—feeling mysteriously enlarged after a sojourn with its rocks, wind, water, and sky.

As President Bill Clinton announced the creation of Grand Staircase–Escalante National Monument at a ceremony on September 18, 1996, cameras panned the colorful canyon country behind him. Strangely, though, this scenery wasn't in the new Utah monument. Instead, it belonged to the Grand Canyon, hundreds of miles to the south in Arizona.

The President had his reasons for going to the Grand Canyon. Long before it became a national park, the Grand Canyon was also protected as a national monument—one of the very first—by Pres. Theodore Roosevelt. The year was 1908, and a brand-new law, the Antiquities Act of 1906, gave Presidents the authority to set aside federal lands of historic or scientific importance as national monuments. Clearly, the Grand Canyon qualified. It was also highly controversial in its day, because Roosevelt's proclamation put the brakes on a variety of mining schemes in and around the canyon. By the same token, Clinton's designation of the Grand Staircase–Escalante National Monument roiled some local residents who feared it might stop development of a huge coal mine on the Kaiparowits Plateau—and the jobs that would come with it.

The new monument was vastly more popular with Americans generally than with southern Utahns—so much so that Clinton was assured a friendlier reception almost anyplace else he cared to proclaim its creation. The setting he chose symbolized the importance of a vision, and a law, to protect outstanding public lands whose value can only multiply over time.

For all the controversy, establishing new national monuments is something that most 20th-century Presidents have done. Teddy Roosevelt and Bill Clinton created the most—Roosevelt 18, Clinton 19. But in between, 11 other Presidents have also named 85 other national monuments. A few are tiny, like the two-acre President Lincoln and Soldier's Home, in Washington, D.C., and some are vast, like Alaska's Wrangell–St. Elias, just shy of 11 million acres. Some eventually have become our favorite national parks—gems like Olympic, or like Zion and Bryce Canyon, next-door neighbors to Grand Staircase.

But there was something altogether new and different about the designation of Grand Staircase: For the first time ever, a new national monument would be run by the BLM. In the past, many of its prize lands were simply

Currents paddled by Lewis and Clark flow around a crescent of land in Montana's Upper Missouri River—designated Wild and Scenic in 1976, part of a new BLM monument since 2001.

FOLLOWING PAGES:

A stairway riser for giants, the Straight Cliffs step upward to the Kaiparowits Plateau in Utah's Grand Staircase–Escalante National Monument, proclaimed in 1996 as the first BLM monument.

turned over to the National Park Service. That had always bothered Bruce Babbitt, Clinton's Secretary of the Interior. He thought the BLM should "have a sense of pride rather than...a bunch of inventory out in the garage that is discovered and given to someone else."

Secretary Babbitt didn't just want BLM to compete with the National Park Service. After all, as Secretary of the Interior, he was in charge of both agencies. Instead, he wanted to transform the BLM—long known to its critics as an industry-dominated Bureau of Livestock and Mining—into a conservation-oriented agency. One of the best ways of doing that, he believed, was to designate some of its most important lands—millions of acres—as national monuments. Although monuments wouldn't necessarily be highly protected from commercial uses, since rules can vary greatly from place to place, Babbitt felt

that the designation would bring these spectacular places attention and visitors, who in turn would demand more protections.

"What brought it into focus was Grand Staircase," says the former secretary of the preparations for creating the new monument in 1996. "I remember the moment, all these years later, when one of the staffers asked, 'Isn't it time to call in the National Park Service?' And I said, 'No, BLM will keep it.' The President had no problem with that.

"I explained to my staff that this was just the beginning," he says. "BLM should keep the lands and reinvent itself as a true conservation agency."

For Clinton, the secretary had an additional message. "The President was a big fan of Teddy Roosevelt," Babbitt says. "I talked to him about Roosevelt's legacy of land conservation and suggested that it was time to think about his own legacy." Clinton, already into his second term in office, agreed. He asked Babbitt for more recommendations for places worthy of designation as national monuments.

One of the first was in Babbitt's home state of Arizona. As a young geology student, he had surveyed parts of the remote Arizona Strip, in the northwest corner of the state, near the Grand Canyon. Later, in 1975, some of the area was nearly included in an expansion of Grand Canyon National Park. But by the late 1990s it was still BLM land—virtually the last unprotected part of the Grand Canyon's watershed. That still bothered Babbitt.

He made several trips to the area—as he would to all BLM lands being considered as national monuments—and met repeatedly with local residents and officials. "Babbitt was the only interior secretary to actually go out in the field and deal directly with managers on the ground," says longtime BLM veteran Roger Taylor, field manager for the 8,400-square-mile Arizona Strip. "And there always had to be a hike, even when he hurt his back. Those hikes weren't just a stroll in the woods, either," Taylor recalls. "They were pretty arduous."

There's little that's not arduous about this rumpled, million-acre landscape—a jumble of canyons, cliffs, mountains, plateaus, plains, and more. There are no paved roads at all, no towns or gas stations. I did see a black Model T pickup in a field, though, grass growing through the rusting hood. It seemed a kind of warning: Two spare tires, or else, was my take on it. But if your luck holds, you can walk amid the ramrod agave stalks of the Mojave Desert and the shady ponderosa groves of breezy plateau lands in a single day. You might also have time to inch, ever so gingerly, out to the edge of Twin Point and stare down thousands of feet, past Surprise and Separation Canyons, into the Lower Granite Gorge of the Grand Canyon. Still, a week or three would serve much better just to explore the highlights—the Grand Wash Cliffs, for starters, a sweeping fault-carved rampart and one of four large wilderness areas in the vicinity. This place has variety enough for a mad master builder, furiously adding and mixing materials.

Still, not everyone was happy when all of this became the new Grand

---

"BLM should have a sense of pride rather than...a bunch of inventory out in the garage that is discovered and given to someone else."

— BRUCE BABBITT, *U.S. Secretary of the Interior, 1993-2001*

Canyon–Parashant National Monument in January 2000. There were, among others, grumblings that the new monument was far bigger than it should have been. But from Bruce Babbitt's point of view, many existing national parks and monuments were much smaller than they needed to be. In fact, the more he looked at how these landmarks were mapped out, the less he liked what he saw. "Grand Canyon National Park was a good example," he says. "The boundaries were very artificial, focusing mainly on the view." Left out was the North Rim's watershed. BLM, he believed, could do better.

"That experience got me looking at maps of the West," Babbitt continues, "and I immediately saw that a lot of National Park Service units had been drawn without a knowledge of conservation biology. Nowadays, biologists tell us that you can't respect the integrity of creation by preserving small 40-acre tracts surrounded by development. If you want to really protect it, you must look at the entire system."

Those same ideas guided Babbitt's thinking about areas rich in archaeological sites—the human environment. "We don't learn about ancient cultures just by digging out a room and finding a few pots," he says. "Ancient people lived in equilibrium with their entire landscape." He has an example at hand:

Agua Fria, just 40 miles from Phoenix, Babbitt's home for years while he was Arizona's governor and attorney general. Hundreds of prehistoric sites and spectacular petroglyphs help make Agua Fria one of the most important treasures of ancient southwestern life. But it's the landscape that completes the story of a community fighting to protect itself on high natural ramparts, locating its watchtowers in a defensive array across nearly 100,000 acres. "It is one of the most complicated, challenging, natural, and human landscapes you can imagine, and right next door to Phoenix," says Babbitt. It makes you think about solitude, he adds, and these days it makes you think about urban sprawl.

New development is galloping out of Arizona's Sunbelt meccas, Phoenix and Tucson, at a rate that makes it likely that much of the hundred-mile desert corridor between those cities will be paved over in a century or two. So it may not be just coincidental that there are three new BLM monuments in the same part of Arizona that's also the fastest-growing—Agua Fria; Ironwood Forest, just north of Tucson; and Sonoran Desert, between Phoenix and Tucson. The "objects of scientific or historic importance" that, under law, qualify lands for protection as national monuments are great there. And so is the need.

If you drew a line on a map going northwest from downtown Tucson, it would soon reach Ironwood Forest National Monument, just 25 miles out of town. In between are expanding suburbs at the edge of town, and beyond, "wildcat" subdivisions, where high demand allows developers to skip amenities like paved streets, curbs and gutters, even sewer lines.

"Urban sprawl is definitely the biggest threat we face here," maintains Carolyn Campbell, head of the Coalition for Sonoran Desert Protection, who has offered to show me around Ironwood Forest one morning. Along with us are Nature Conservancy biologist Dale Turner and geologist Julia Fonseca. The morning's banner headline in the Arizona *Daily Star* has already set the stage for the outing with an article about local birds: "...Native Species Driven to Outskirts." Along the way, Turner tells me that new homes have also pushed bighorn sheep out of the Tucson foothills.

As usual in the BLM's new national monuments, we seem to have all 129,000 acres of rolling desert and ragged mountains to ourselves. Still, it's noisy here. Trills, chirps, cackles, and whistles fill the air, and this Sonoran sonata doesn't even include the voices of some of its best known birds, including an endangered pygmy owl. If you closed your eyes and opened

Light-stepping pack goats, favored for their low impact on fragile environments, trail an out-
fitter across the Honeycomb Buttes in southwestern Wyoming's Red Desert. Despite its shifting dunes, wildlife, and undeveloped high desert, this region never won federal protection.

your ears, you might imagine yourself in a lush, mature forest. And you would be right, even though it might not look that way at first.

Of all the deserts in the world, the Sonoran, stretching from central Arizona into northern Mexico, is the richest. And Ironwood, measured by the plants and animals that make their home there, boasts some of the richest of the rich. Holding it all together—the tree of life here—is the humbly magnificent ironwood, which only grows in the Sonoran desert.

"If you're thinking in terms of soaring California redwoods, this doesn't look like great old growth, does it?" biologist Turner asks. Indeed not. Before us stands a halo of tiny, dark, grayish-green leaves perched above a pair of gnarly, branching trunks. To the untrained eye, it's a slightly scraggly, 25-foot evergreen—but to the denizens of the Sonoran Desert, it's an oasis. "It's an island of fertility over many centuries," says Turner; ironwoods can live up to 1,500 years. "Whole generations of plants and animals depend on them."

Thorns halo a cholla cactus in Arizona, where three of BLM's new national monuments—Sonoran Desert, Ironwood Forest, and Agua Fria—enclose the unique plants and animals of the world's most species-rich desert, the Sonoran.

Nearly 150 bird species nest or roost in their dense canopies. Under the canopies spreads a circle of shade that is much cooler than the surrounding desert in summer, and less likely to frost over in winter. Bighorn sheep forage there; tortoises burrow there. Hundreds of different plants—including giant saguaros, the Sonoran emblem—get their start in those charmed circles. For the native peoples who have lived in the area for 5,000 years, the ironwoods are both a pharmacy and a food supply. Writes ethnobotanist Gary Nabhan, who has studied the trees for years, "The list of residents living under a 45-foot ironwood reads like the Who's Who of the Sonoran Desert."

But the list of conflicting uses—mining, grazing, and off-road vehicles—is a long one too, as it is on many BLM lands, including the new national monuments. There, existing commercial leases generally continue, though new mining and drilling leasing may be stopped. As we slowly circle a huge, ancient ironwood, he points to a low-spreading plant beyond its shade. "This little bursage could be 50 years old." Then to a brushy, angular shrub. "This creosote could be many centuries old." The ironwood itself is no doubt even older. "People usually don't think these are important when they drive over them or cut them down," he says. "All of these are our elders."

A wish to preserve something ancient and fundamentally important—but little known or long ignored—was the starting point for several of the 15 new BLM national monuments. Some of them had been on conservationists' radar for decades; Santa Rosa and San Jacinto Mountains National Monument, in California's Mojave Desert, for instance, was proposed as a national park in the 1920s. But even Bruce Babbitt had never heard of Carrizo Plain, to the north.

On the edge of the San Joaquin Valley, this 200,000-acre monument holds the last large remnant of the vast sea of grass that once swept across central California. It is a wild, elemental place, where the San Andreas Fault slashes across the earth's surface between California's coastal ranges. Just 50 miles east of San Luis Obispo, the Carrizo Plain can seem centuries away from modern California. "It's one of the only places you can still go to get away from people," says Johna Hurl, the monument's manager. Her office is so remote that generators provide electricity and cell phones, the only communication.

Long ago, the native Chumash and Yokut people hunted on Carrizo Plain's game-rich grasslands. But later, when Spanish missionaries brought in livestock herds, the slow, relentless destruction of native grasses began. In the 20th century, dry land grain farmers plowed under much of the rest. By then, hunting had already eliminated the native elk and antelope. Still, the landscape the Spaniards called Llano Estero—salt marsh plain—has remained big enough to hold healthy ecosystems. In winter, the skies over its alkali wetlands fill with sandhill cranes and curlews. Kit foxes, coyotes, kangaroo rats, and other animals burrow away from summer heat. And at any time of year, Carrizo Plain holds more endangered plants and animals than anyplace else in California.

But there are big gaps. To start filling them, restoration of the historical landscape is taking many forms. Reintroduced, herds of tule elk and pronghorn antelope browse here once again. Condors, long near the brink of extinction, glide overhead on impossibly broad wingspans. Restoration is not just nostalgia, though. Carrizo Plain is, for instance, one of the few safe places left in the state for large soaring birds. Already, the San Joaquin Valley itself is the nation's top agricultural region, and one of its most populous. As more common creatures of the San Joaquin Valley continue losing ground to farming and development, the plain will have to become more of a haven for them, too.

You get a strong sense of change on the doorstep of many of the new national monuments, even remote ones. But not all. And I also visited places, few though, that seemed untouched by the passage of centuries. One of them was the Missouri River in north-central Montana, bordered by the towering bluffs and badlands of the new Upper Missouri Breaks National Monument. There, one evening, I beached my canoe to make camp and watch the sun set on the White Cliffs, a stone's throw across the flat water. As the light played itself out on its dazzling sandstone face, I compared notes with the Cliffs' earliest chronicler, explorer Meriwether Lewis, whose Corps of Discovery camped here on May 31, 1805.

"The hills and river Clifts...exhibit a most romantic appearance," Lewis began. Carved by trickling water, they reminded him of "a thousand grotesque figures." There were "eligant ranges of lofty freestone buildings" and ruins,"some collumns standing and almost entire with their pedestals and capitals...othe[r]s in the form of vast pyramids.... As we passed on it

FOLLOWING PAGES:

A forest of tapering cones bristles across New Mexico's Kasha-Katuwe Tent Rocks National Monument, where erosion chisels rock formations formed by volcanic eruption.

Discoveries still abound on Alaska's remote BLM lands. Near Lonely, Alaska, on the Beaufort Sea, a skull suddenly comes to light—likely the remains of a sailor on a 19th-century whaler, stranded by weather and done in by lead poisoning from canned rations. Below, surveyors delivered by helicopter stake the Tangle Lakes area.

seemed as if those seens of visionary inchantment would never have and [an] end...so perfect indeed are those walls."

Two centuries later, Lewis's words ring true. As in the Corps of Discovery's day, the preferred way to see the miles of dazzling cliffs is by small boat. Quite a few people do, the BLM says, though I saw just a half dozen or so other canoes on the river near the White Cliffs. Downstream, the next day, there was no one at all near Citadel Rock, a soaring black finger of igneous rock that pointed the way west for Lewis and Clark; no one as I paddled on toward the stream that Lewis named Slaughter Creek for the stinking carcasses of bison, drowned in an ice breakup, that he saw piled high there.

More than 30 miles of solitude separate that site, now called Arrow
Creek, from the rugged bluffs near Bullwhacker Creek, beyond the White
Cliffs. There, Clark and Lewis caught their first glimpses of the snowcapped
Rocky Mountains, bathed in sunshine. The view triggered joy—and appre-
hension—for Clark, for "the difficulties which this snowy barrier would
most probably throw in my way to the Pacific [Ocean]."

It was near there that Lewis would spy "several gangs" of bighorn sheep and
introduce his fellow Americans to them with a detailed description. He marveled
at the way they would "bound from rock to rock and stand apparently in the most
careless manner on the sides of precipices of many hundred feet." The next day

he killed a bison for food—and a rattlesnake that lay inches from his feet. The bison are long gone, but rattlesnakes are abundant, and bighorn sheep still scamper across some of the wildest, most remote public land anywhere in the lower 48. A stretch of river past the White Cliffs includes several areas eligible for wilderness designation. But all 149 miles of the national monument, to the edge of the Great Plains, far downstream, are a wondrous anomaly. They represent the last undeveloped stretch of the entire Missouri River, more than 2,000 miles long, which now mostly flows through landscapes dramatically transformed since Lewis and Clark made it the nation's first highway to the west.

When it comes to the fate of some of the most spectacular landscapes in the nation, both sides—all sides—view the BLM differently.

As you canoe through the Monument, the loudest sound is usually the dip and splash of your own paddle in the water. But in the region's small towns, on its cattle ranches and wheat farms, mention of the new BLM monument was still raising voices at the time of my visit—several months after the ink on the proclamation creating it had dried. "When we asked people what they wanted, everybody talked about wildness and how much they want to keep it," says rancher Hugo Tureck, chairman of a council formed to solicit Montanans' opinions on the future of the Missouri Breaks before the Monument was created. "But that's about all everyone had managed to agree on." From one camp came complaints about more government, more rules, more employees, more tourists, more unwanted change—real or imagined. From another came insistence that change was necessary because of agriculture's struggles; that the monument would help the local economy; that the Missouri Breaks deserve more and better protection. A new round of local town-hall-type meetings was underway, even though Presidents and the Congress have so seldom tried to tamper with national monuments during the last century that many legal scholars now question their right to do so.

Adding to the confusion, different monuments can be run in vastly different ways. New monuments land in the national spotlight, and that usually puts more emphasis on conservation, says Joe Feller, a public lands expert at Arizona State University's law school. "But both sides like to exaggerate the significance of formal recognition," he adds. "The BLM has a lot of discretion."

When it comes to the fate of some of the most spectacular landscapes in the nation, both sides—all sides—view the BLM differently. Environmentalists wonder about BLM's ability to sensitively manage the legacy that Bruce Babbitt named the National Landscape Conservation System in 2000; in addition to the new national monuments, it includes BLM's national conservation areas, wilderness-quality lands, and thousands of miles of Wild and Scenic Rivers and National Historic Trails. To traditional public lands permit holders like ranchers and energy companies, the agency seemed like an old friend undergoing a strange personality change during the Clinton years—though it started acting more like its old user-friendly self under the succeeding Republican administration, which has vigorously promoted oil and gas drilling in several new national monuments, including Upper Missouri Breaks.

"We've always been more subject to shifting political winds than other land agencies are, and so we get pushed back and forth depending on who's in the White House," says one BLM manager. No place proves his point better than Alaska, with some 85 million acres of BLM-managed land.

Everyplace else, the law requires BLM to study its vast holdings for areas pristine enough to qualify as protected, roadless wilderness where new development of any kind is permanently banned. And over the years, BLM has done so, though usually halfheartedly. Today, the largest protected wilderness areas—millions of acres—are in California's Mojave Desert. There are also dozens of Wilderness Study Areas awaiting congressional approval. But a quirk of law altogether sidesteps Alaska, where the secretary of the interior decides whether to study an area's wilderness potential. James Watt, in that office under Pres. Ronald Reagan, blocked wilderness inventories from ever starting up. Because Alaska's BLM lands have not been studied, no one knows what's out

FOLLOWING PAGES:

Blazing sunset leaves in shadow the famous gap in Kiger Gorge, atop Oregon's Steens Mountain. Bulldozing down to basalt, Ice Age glaciers carved four huge gorges out of the Great Basin's largest fault block mountain. Beyond, Steens's east face plummets a vertical mile.

there. A successor, Bruce Babbitt, finally reversed that decision in 2001.

But where to begin in this vastness? Babbitt himself mentioned the Colville River, the longest river on the great North Slope. For 428 miles, the Colville snakes from the Brooks Range, through the 23.5-million-acre National Petroleum Reserve Alaska (NPRA)—BLM's biggest holding in the state by far—and meanders on across the Arctic coastal plain until it empties into the Beaufort Sea, west of Prudhoe Bay.

I haven't gotten there yet. Only a few balmy weeks—weeks I had to be elsewhere—separate ice breakup from the stirrings of early winter. Go too soon in June, and you risk an encounter with a hungry polar bear floating on an ice patch at the Colville's mouth. Go too late, in August, and you risk a colder kind of misery. Then there are logistical hangups, like arranging to fly rafts—and everything else you need for a week in the backcountry—in on a small plane, and you sigh as your thoughts turn to next year.

I think it'll be worth the wait, though, to hear thousands of songbirds in the shrublands along the river. I'd like to lie back in my raft and stare up at the high bluffs where falcons, hawks, and Canada geese nest. I'm eager to glimpse brown bear, wolves, wolverines, moose, muskox, foxes, caribou, and maybe even polar bear—from a safe distance—as I float past.

But I wouldn't want to wait too long to make this trip. Until 2000, the Colville corridor held only two tiny native villages. Now, there's a third—buzzing with hundreds of employees, roaring with turbines—that serves the new alpine oilfield in the Colville River Delta as it pumps 80,000 gallons a day from the tundra. Rigs are also probing the NPRA to the west. Off to the east is the Arctic National Wildlife Refuge. Oil companies are eager to show that they can drill in the refuge without harming it, and BLM lands along the Colville may be the laboratory for the ongoing experiment.

I haven't floated through this landscape myself, though I know people who have. None of them know all the wonders there—or elsewhere in BLM's Alaskan lands—and neither will the BLM's people until they study it. But I have a pretty strong hunch that this sounds like wilderness, untouched enough to

Horseback riders cross the Alvord Desert, a huge expanse of playa, salt desert scrub, sand dunes, and hot springs in the arid rain shadow of Steens Mountain. As ecologically distinct as Steens, the Alvord Desert boasts nearly 300,000 acres of potential BLM wilderness.

Land yachts race the wind, and each other, across the Alvord playa's flatness. Fans of the sport flock to the ancient lake bed in search of speeds beyond most posted interstate highway limits; the world record stands above 116 miles per hour. Determination counts for much with yachtsmen (and women), who travel hours to this isolated corner of south-eastern Oregon and contend with extreme heat in summer, the only season when the playa is reliably dry enough for sailing.

qualify as a disappearing rarity in today's world. As the conservationist Aldo Leopold said, "Wilderness is a resource that can shrink but not grow."

A cowboy's tears are not something you see every day. Neither are some other sights and sounds and smells around me on a stiflingly hot morning at a small BLM campground in remote southeastern Oregon. Two United States Senators, for instance, one Democratic, one Republican. A U.S. Congressman (Republican). Sleek Stetsons and BLM baseball caps with the river in the logo; Teva sandals and dress boots. There is children's laughter in the distance. The plaintive, urgent cadence of a prayer in the language of the Paiute tribe, whose land this once was, floating above the

Children of the Davies family turn ranch cattle chute into their homegrown playground on the Roaring Springs Ranch, near Steens Mountain. Mending fences has not always been an easy matter for their father, ranch manager Stacy Davies (below, with his son), who represented landowners in negotiations over Steens's future. In the end, all compromised. In complex land exchanges, ranchers gained public acreage as private land—more than 60,000 acres in the case of Roaring Springs Ranch.

crowd. The rich fragrance of barbecue wafting in on a cloud of smoke.

There's a whiff of something else in the air as well—compromise. This gathering is the dedication of the Steens Mountain Cooperative Management and Protection Area, an eye-glazing name for a one-of-a-kind place; a name that only hints at the complexity of compromise and the distances traveled to reach it.

At the podium, the man with tears on his sunburned cheeks is Stacy Davies, manager of the Roaring Springs Ranch. Times are changing and the future is uncertain, says Davies, representing the landowners in the Steens Mountain discussions. "Our ancestors made some ecological decisions that weren't the best, and we have had to adapt." Among the adaptations his side signed off on: creation of the first legislated livestock-free wilderness area in the United States, almost 100,000 acres. To create a congruous wilderness area, public land was traded for private. Ranchers gained tens of thousands of former BLM acres as private land, and a big say in running the new Steens Mountain CMPA. "We all had to step out of our respective comfort zones to make this work," notes Jill Workman, the conservationists' representative.

Still, adds Andy Kerr, another environmentalist, "If you're a bighorn sheep or a sage grouse, you're very happy with those land exchanges." And there's more in this package, wrapped and beribboned in that long name. There are, among other things, several new Wild and Scenic Rivers, bans on off-road vehicles, a special reserve for rare redband trout.

It almost turned out quite differently. People have long known that Steens Mountain deserved special recognition; anyone who sees this sky island floating above the surrounding Alvord Desert senses that this is a place apart. But how to manage it, and for whom? People argued fiercely about Steens's future. Finally, in the waning days of the Clinton administration, Interior Secretary Babbitt mentioned the controversial M-word. With a stroke of his pen, he warned, the President might just create one. As he tells it, after a group hike on the mountain, "I told everyone that I was prepared to recommend Steens as a national monument. Nothing would've happened without that stick." What happened instead, as Babbitt himself predicted it might, was a locally driven plan for protecting Steens that eventually worked its way through Congress.

"It was clear that people here wanted a homegrown approach," says U.S. Senator Randy Wyden of Oregon, at the Steens festivities. "We hope we can serve as a model for other places." Americans as a whole can hope so, too.

But after a morning full of words, it is time to go let the mountain speak for itself. So I take the North Loop Road toward the summit, to spend the rest of the day amid Steens's silent splendors. It's a serious uphill slog. This 30-mile-long Ice Age wonder—one of the continent's largest fault blocks—rises a mile above the surrounding landscape. Formidable enough to make its own precipitation, Steens is big enough to hold eight different life zones, each with signature wildlife. You pass through stands of mountain mahogany and quaking aspens, sagebrush steppes below and late summer snowdrifts above. Steens's mountaintop tundra is unique in the Great Basin. Near the summit, well above treeline, I hike out on a ridge for a

Skipping stones breaks up a day hike on Steens Mountain. "We constantly work against the Marlboro Man myth," says longtime resident and trip leader Alice Elshoff, at right. Environmentalists like Elshoff cheered the creation of BLM's first cattle-free wilderness at Steens.

FOLLOWING PAGES:

On a collision course with a thunderstorm, headlights pierce the darkness atop Steens Mountain.

glimpse at Wildhorse Lake. It's probably 25 degrees cooler than it was at the campground, but the altitude—almost 10,000 feet—takes my breath away.

Maybe it's not just the altitude. Steens's half-mile-deep U-shaped gorges and hanging valleys and wild rivers and wild mustangs are sights than can knock the wind right out of you. So can the view straight down a full mile to the blindingly white, utterly flat Alvord Playa, another world of public land, stretching out past the horizon. As I stare out over the playa, fragments of past conversations break the silence—the voices of people speaking and arguing so passionately about the fate of Steens and of many other peerless places in the public domain. In my mind, I also hear the occasional voice that still calls them leftover lands, or scraps, or places no one wanted. That will always take my breath away. ■

ADDITIONAL INFORMATION

In addition to the National Conservation Areas and National Monuments listed below, BLM's National Landscape Conservation System includes 11 National Scenic and Historic Trails; 148 Wilderness Areas; 604 Wilderness Study Areas, and portions of 36 Wild and Scenic Rivers.

NATIONAL CONSERVATION AREAS

(Dates of congressional designation appear in parentheses.)

BLACK ROCK DESERT–HIGH ROCK CANYON EMIGRANT TRAILS
(December 21, 2000) This area includes nearly 800,000 acres in northwestern Nevada and protects wagon ruts, historic inscriptions, and a wilderness landscape largely unchanged from the 1800s.

CALIFORNIA DESERT
(October 21, 1976) This area's 10.6 million acres feature vast desert areas with wildlife and recreational opportunities.

COLORADO CANYONS
(October 24, 2000) From saltbush desert to the canyons of the Black Ridge Wilderness, this area in west-central Colorado includes more than 122,000 acres, 75,000 of wilderness.

EL MALPAIS
(December 31, 1987) These 226,000 acres of lava flows in west-central New Mexico include geological, cultural, scenic, scientific, and wilderness sites.

GILA BOX RIPARIAN
(November 28, 1990) This 22,000-acre desert oasis in southeastern Arizona contains cliff dwellings, historic homesteads, Rocky Mountain bighorn sheep, and more than 200 species of birds.

GUNNISON GORGE
October 21, 1999) Western Colorado's Gunnison Gorge,, a 57,725-acre area, includes a variety of natural and geologic features and supports a diverse range of uses such as whitewater rafting, big-game hunting, and domestic livestock grazing.

HEADWATERS FOREST RESERVE
(March 1, 1999) These 7,400 acres in northern California protect old-growth redwoods and threatened species such as the marbled murrelet and coho salmon.

KING RANGE
(October 21, 1970) West of Arcata, 35 miles of remote coastline comprise the 57,000-acre King Range, the nation's first National Conservation Area.

LAS CIENEGAS
(December 6, 2000) These 42,000 acres of desert grasslands and rolling hills in south-central Arizona support diverse plant and animal life, including threatened or endangered species.

RED ROCK CANYON
(November 16, 1990) This 197,000-acre area outside of Las Vegas displays geologic features, plants, and animals—some of the best examples of the Mojave Desert.

SAN PEDRO RIPARIAN
(November 18, 1988) This 56,500-acre area in southeastern Arizona supports over 350 species of birds, 80 species of mammals, and 40 species of amphibians and reptiles.

SNAKE RIVER BIRDS OF PREY
(August 4, 1993) Home to the largest concentration of nesting raptors in North America, this 485,000-acre area in southwestern Idaho provides a stable ecosystem for both predators and prey.

STEENS MOUNTAIN
(October 30, 2000) Officially the Steens Mountain Cooperative Management and Protection Area, these 425,500 acres in southeastern Oregon include volcanic uplifts, glacier-carved gorges, wild rivers, and diverse plant and animal species.

STEESE

(December 2, 1980) This 1.2-million-acre area in east-central Alaska contains a Wild and Scenic River, crucial caribou calving grounds, and Dall sheep habitat.

SONORAN DESERT

(January 17, 2001) Wide valleys separated by rugged mountain ranges offer dense forests of saguaro cactus—excellent habitat for many species—in this 409,000-acre area in southwestern Arizona.

UPPER MISSOURI RIVER BREAKS

(January 17, 2001) The breathtaking limestone bluffs along this 149-mile, 377,000-acre stretch of Missouri River in central Montana remain almost exactly the same as when Lewis and Clark described them in their expedition journals.

VERMILION CLIFFS

(November 9, 2000) An outstanding assemblage of deep, narrow canyons makes the 280,000 acres in this northern Arizona Monument ideal for hiking and exploring.

NATIONAL MONUMENTS

AGUA FRIA

(January 11, 2000) An hour north of Phoenix, Agua Fria's 71,000 acres host one of the most significant systems of late prehistoric sites in the American Southwest.

CALIFORNIA COASTAL

(January 11, 2000) This national monument includes all the islands, rocks, and pinnacles off the 840-mile California coast, habitat for an estimated 200,000 breeding seabirds.

CANYONS OF THE ANCIENTS

(June 9, 2000) Located in southwestern Colorado, this 163,000-acre area contains the richest known concentration of archaeological sites in the United States.

CARRIZO PLAIN

(January 17, 2001) Remnant of a once-vast grassland astride the San Andreas Fault zone, this unit's 204,000 acres in central California harbor several endangered and threatened animal and plant species.

CASCADE–SISKIYOU

(June 9, 2000) The convergence of geologically young and old mountain ranges gives this 53,000- acre monument in south-central Oregon an extraordinary degree of biological diversity.

CRATERS OF THE MOON

(November 9, 2000) The 272,000 acres of this remarkably preserved volcanic landscape on Idaho's Snake River Plain contain an array of features, including cinder cones and vast lava fields.

GRAND CANYON–PARASHANT

(January 11, 2000) This 808,000-acre area in northwestern Arizona contains outstanding geological and paleontological features.

GRAND STAIRCASE-ESCALANTE

(September 19, 1996) Labyrinthine redrock canyons, high plateaus, cliffs, and terraces make up this 1.9- million-acre area in southern Utah.

IRONWOOD FOREST

(June 9, 2000) This 129,000-acre area protects a unique ironwood forest and a wide array of bird and animal life in southern Arizona.

KASHA–KATUWE TENT ROCKS

(January 17, 2001) This area in northern New Mexico protects over 4,000 acres of cone-shaped rock formations, the result of volcanic eruptions and erosion that first built up, then wore down this landscape.

POMPEYS PILLAR

(January 17, 2001) William Clark of the Lewis and Clark Expedition carved his name on this sandstone butte overlooking the Yellowstone River, adding to the record of historic inscriptions now protected as a 51-acre area in central Montana.

SANTA ROSA AND SAN JACINTO MOUNTAINS

(October 24, 2000) This 86,500-acre National Monument in southern California hosts over 500 plant and animal species, including the federally listed Peninsular bighorn sheep.

BLM OFFICES

ALASKA
State Director Henry Bisson
222 West 7th Avenue, #13
Anchorage, AK 99513-7599
(907) 271-5960

ARIZONA
State Director Elaine Zielinski
222 North Central Ave.
Phoenix, AZ 85004-2203
(602) 417-9300

CALIFORNIA
State Director Mike Pool
2800 Cottage Way, Room W-1834
Sacramento, CA 95825
(916) 978-4400

COLORADO
State Director Ann Morgan
2850 Youngfield Street
Lakewood, CO 80215-7093
(303) 239-3600

EASTERN STATES OFFICE
State Director Mike Nedd
7450 Boston Blvd.
Springfield, VA 22153
(703) 440-1600

IDAHO
Acting State Director Mike Ferguson
1387 S. Vinnell Way
Boise, Idaho 83709-1657
(208) 373-3889

MONTANA
Acting State Director Sherry Barnett
5001 Southgate Street
Billings, MT 59101
(406) 896-5004

NEVADA
State Director Bob Abbey
1340 Financial Way
Reno, NV 89502
(775) 861-6500

NEW MEXICO
Acting State Director Chuck Wassinger
1474 Rodeo Rd.
P.O. Box 27115
Santa Fe, NM 87502-0115
(505) 438-7400

OREGON
State Director Elaine Brong
P.O. Box 2965
Portland, OR 97208-2965
(503) 952-6001

UTAH
State Director Sally Wisely
324 South State Street
P.O. Box 45155
Salt Lake City, UT 84145-0155
(801) 539-4230

WYOMING
State Director Al Pierson
5353 Yellowstone Road
P.O. Box 1828
Cheyenne, WY 82003
(307) 775-6011

ABOUT THE AUTHOR AND PHOTOGRAPHER

LESLIE ALLEN, a former National Geographic staff writer, writes on nature, the environment, and American social history for the *New York Times*, *Smithsonian*, and other publications. She is the author of *Liberty: The Statue and the American Dream*. Raised in Latin America, she lives in the Washington, D.C., area.

MELISSA FARLOW has photographed for National Geographic for more than 12 years—from the Okefenokee Swamp to the Pan-American Highway. She was part of the Louisville *Courier-Journal* photographic team awarded a Pulitzer Prize for coverage of school desegregation. She lives in Sewickley, Pennsylvania.

ADDITIONAL READING

Abbey, Edward. *Desert Solitaire.* Ballantine Books, 1971.

Abbey, Edward. *The Monkey Wrench Gang.* J. B. Lippincott, 1975.

Ambrose, Stephen E. *Undaunted Courage: Meriwether Lewis, Thomas Jefferson, and the Opening of the American West.* Simon and Schuster, 1996.

Clawson, Marion. *The Land System of the United States: An Introduction to the History and Practice of Land Use and Land Tenure.* University of Nebraska Press, 1972.

Chesher, Greer K. *Heart of the Desert Wild: Grand Staircase–Escalante National Monument.* Bryce Canyon Natural History Association, 2000.

Crossette, George, ed. *Selected Prose of John Wesley Powell.* David R. Godine, 1970.

DeVoto, Bernard. *The Easy Chair.* Houghton Mifflin, 1955.

Egan, Timothy. *Lasso the Wind.* Alfred A. Knopf, 1998.

Fisher, Ron. *Our Threatened Inheritance: Natural Treasures of the United States.* National Geographic Society, 1984

Hunt, Charles B. *Natural Regions of the United States and Canada.* W. H. Freeman and Company, 1974.

Kerr, Andy. *Oregon Desert Guide: 70 Hikes.* Mountaineers, 2000.

Leopold, Aldo. *A Sand County Almanac.* Ballantine Books, 1978.

Meine, Curt, and Richard L. Knight, eds. *The Essential Aldo Leopold: Quotations and Commentaries.* University of Wisconsin Press, 1999.

Peffer, E. Louise. *The Closing of the Public Domain: Disposal and Reservation Policies 1900-1950.* Stanford University Press, 1951.

Riebsame, William, ed. *Atlas of the New West: Portrait of a Changing Region.* W.W. Norton, 1997.

Ricketts, Taylor H., et al. *Terrestrial Ecoregions of North America: A Conservation Assessment.* Island Press, 1999.

Stegner, Wallace. *Beyond the Hundredth Meridian: John Wesley Powell and the Second Opening of the West.* Houghton Mifflin, 1954.

Stegner, Wallace. *Where the Bluebird Sings to the Lemonade Springs: Living and Writing in the West.* Random House, 1992.

Stegner, Wallace, and Wayne Owens. *Wilderness at the Edge: A Citizen Proposal to Protect Utah's Canyons and Deserts.* Utah Wilderness Coalition, 1991.

Tisdale, Mary E., and Bibi Booth, eds. *Beyond the National Parks: A Recreation Guide to Public Lands in the West.* Smithsonian Institution Press, 1998.

Trimble, Stephen. *The Sagebrush Ocean: A Natural History of the Great Basin.* University of Nevada Press, 1989.

Watkins, T. H., and Charles Watson. *The Lands No One Knows: America and the Public Domain.* Sierra Club Books, 1975.

Wilcove, David S. *The Condor's Shadow: The Loss and Recovery of Wildlife in America.* W. H. Freeman, 1999.

Wilkinson, Charles F. *Crossing the Next Meridian: Land, Water, and the Future of the West.* Island Press, 1992.

Zaslowsky, Dyan, and T. H. Watkins. *These American Lands.* The Wilderness Society, 1986.

In addition, NATIONAL GEOGRAPHIC, *National Wildlife, Wilderness, Sierra, Nature Conservancy, High Country News,* and various other publications include many articles on issues relating to public lands. The Bureau of Land Management itself is the source of a multitude of high-quality publications.

INDEX

ACKNOWLEDGMENTS

In addition to those individuals mentioned in the text, all of whom freely shared their time and energy, the author and photographer wish to acknowledge: Dave Alberswerth, Arden Anderson, Fletcher Anderson, John Anderson, Sandy Anderson, Mark Armstrong, Jerry Asher, Victoria Atkins, LouAnn Jacobsen Ball, Lynn Ballard, Ben Beach, Jan Bedrosian, Bob Beehler, Noah Bigwood, Mac Blewer, Celia Boddington, Ed Bovy, Craig Bromley, Bob Brown, Nathan Burkpile, Tana Chattin, Jack Connelly, Bob Connery, Stacey Davies, Diane Dropka, Alice and Cal Elshoff, Richard Flanders, Susan Flora, Gregory Foote, Michele Gangaware, Craig Gehrke, Jim Graham, Ken Greenberger, J. Kent Hamilton, Hal Halburn, Lisa Hathaway, Inter Agency Fire Center, Catherine Johnson, Joel Kerley, John Keys, James Kirkland, Kate Kitchell, Bart Koehler, Jeff Krauss, Ferron Leavitt, Jim Leffmann, *Lighthawk*, Tom Lustig, Wes Martel, Craig McCaa, Mike McCurry, Herb McHarg and Amy Irvine, Mike Miller, Shaaron Netherton, Julie Palette, Glen Pardy, Cheryl Phinney, Dan Randolph, Heidi Redd, Ross Rice, Barry Rose, Jeff Rose, Jeanine Rossa and Paul Hosten, Mike Salamacha, Jeff Scott, Greg Schaefer, Alan Septoff, Gary Slagel, Mike Small, Don Sorensen, Mark Squillace, Gary Starbuck, Sue Steinacher, Roger Taylor, Liz Thomas, Alan Titus, Brian Von Herzen, Bill Wagers, Eric Walter, Charles Watson, Terri Watson, Jay Watson, Jeff Widen, Dave Willis, Charlie Wilson, Sharon Wilson, John Winnepennix, Wendell Wood, Keith Woodworth, Maggie Wyatt, Denny Wyman. A special thanks to Randy Olson, Rich Newton, Pat Tehan, Rebecca Perry, Dennis Dimick, John Mitchell, Kathy Moran, Bert Fox, and Kent Kobersteen. We would also like to thank former National Geographic staffers Tom Melham and John Agnone for getting this book off to a great start.

Wildlands of the West: The Story of the Bureau of Land Management

By Leslie Allen

Photographed by Melissa Farlow

Published by the National Geographic Society

John M. Fahey, Jr.,
President and Chief Executive Officer

Gilbert M. Grosvenor, *Chairman of the Board*

Nina D. Hoffman, *Executive Vice President*

Prepared by the Book Division

Kevin Mulroy, *Vice President and Editor-in-Chief*

Charles Kogod, *Illustrations Director*

Marianne R. Koszorus, *Design Director*

Staff for this Book

Dale-Marie Herring, *Editor*

Rebecca Barns, Susan Tyler Hitchcock, *Contributing Editors*

Charles Kogod, *Illustrations Editor*

David Griffin, *Art Director*

Eleanor Stables, *Researcher*

Carl Mehler, *Director of Maps*

Gary Colbert, *Production Director*

Rick Wain, *Production Project Manager*

Meredith Wilcox, *Illustrations Assistant*

Manufacturing and Quality Control

Christopher A. Liedel, *Chief Financial Officer*

Phillip L. Schlosser, *Managing Director*

John T. Dunn, *Technical Director*

Vincent P. Ryan, *Manager*

Clifton M. Brown, *Manager*

Library of Congress Cataloging-in-Publication Data is available upon request.

"The Wave" laps gently at a footprint-size pool of indigo in the redrock wilderness of Vermilion Cliffs National Monument, where topsy-turvy labyrinths of sandstone abound.